LEAPFROG
PUBLIC ACCOUNTING'S LEARNING CURVE

Leapfrog Public Accounting's Learning Curve:
Real Life Advice for New Hire Success

Copyright © 2020 by Thomas Dunbar

All rights reserved. No portion of this book may be reproduced, stored in a retrieval system, or transmitted in any form or by any means—electronic, mechanical, photocopy, recording, scanning, or other—without the prior written permission of the publisher.

Print ISBN: 978-1-7346269-0-2
E-book ISBN: 978-1-7346269-1-9

Visual credits: jumping frog (Aleksandr Sulga/Shutterstock.com); office workers (Nadia Snopek/Shutterstock.com); page border (Tartila/Shutterstock.com).

Editing by: Brian Baker
Design by: David Miles

LEAPFROG

PUBLIC ACCOUNTING'S LEARNING CURVE

Real Life Advice for New Hire Success

THOMAS DUNBAR, CPA, CFE

CONTENTS

Acknowledgments 7

Chapter 1: "We Assume You Suck" 11

SECTION 1: FIRM HIERARCHIES 17

Chapter 2: Your Firm's Hierarchy 19

SECTION 2: INTERPERSONAL SKILLS 25

Chapter 3: The First Impression 27

Chapter 4: Attributes of Great Associates 33

Chapter 5: Attributes of Substandard Associates 55

Chapter 6: Likeability Best Practices 73

Chapter 7: How to Talk to Clients and Coworkers 81

SECTION 3: CHEAT CODES AND CAREER ADVICE 93

Chapter 8: The Right Firm Fit for Your Life 95

Chapter 9: Résumés and Interviewing 107

Chapter 10: Workplace Best Practices 115

Chapter 11: Setting and Pursuing Goals 135

Chapter 12: Studying for the CPA Exams 141

Chapter 13: The CFE and Other Certifications 153

SECTION 4: GLOSSARY AND FAREWELL..................................159

Glossary: Lingo You Did Not Hear In School 161

Farewell 189

ACKNOWLEDGMENTS

I would like to publicly thank the following people for making this book possible:

My parents, Mary and Tom Dunbar

My siblings, Mary M. and Wirt Dunbar

My grandparents, Mary and Wirt Yerger

My editor, Brian Baker

My designer, David Miles

All of my former and current bosses and coworkers

All of my former teachers and professors

All of my former coaches and teammates

Finally, I would like to thank the following friends who helped guide me through the publishing process: Anderson Baldy, Suzanne Marrs, Joe Maxwell, Dr. Darden North, and Weston Russ.

The author has taken extreme caution in writing this book. However, he assumes no responsibility for errors, omissions, or for any damages resulting from the use of the information and opinions contained herein. The information, opinions, advice, and strategies found within may not be suitable for every situation. This work is sold with the understanding that neither the author nor the publisher are held responsible for the results accrued from the information, opinions, advice, and strategies found in this book.

CHAPTER 1

"WE ASSUME YOU SUCK"

Thank you for your purchase of *Leapfrog Public Accounting's Learning Curve: Real Life Advice for New Hire Success.* Whether you are already in a practice or only considering a career in audit, tax, or advisory, the fact that you bought this book tells me that you have what it takes to be successful in public accounting. I hope you enjoy this read and find my thoughts and opinions helpful.

In the accounting world people often say that it takes a new entry-level hire six to ten months to fully understand what is going on at the firm and to operate at the level expected of an average employee. I will readily admit it took me at least that long to reach a proficient level. This book was written to shorten the new hire learning curve and set you up for massive success as you progress in your career. I want to say up front that almost nothing in this book is technical or is taught in school. There will be no discussions of debits and credits, tax codification, or accounting guidance. Instead, this book is focused entirely on other areas that new hires need to master in order to experience massive success in the early stages of their public accounting careers. My hope is that the few hours you spend reading this book will result in months of saved time and energy on the job.

This book is specifically targeted for students interested in public accounting, recent graduates set on joining a practice, and new associates and interns. I want to convey knowledge that is essential for your success as a new hire, but which was probably not taught to you through your academic accounting education. I realized during my first few years in the workforce that there are mandatory skills and behavior patterns needed for success at work which are not taught in accounting classrooms. Academic accounting studies can provide a fantastic foundation for success in public accounting, but a supplemental, non-technical skill-set is needed once the starting gun sounds and the rat race begins. I majored in Accounting and Business Administration at Washington and Lee University and received a Master in Accounting at the University of Texas at Austin. Washington and Lee graduates secured the highest CPA pass rate of any U.S. institution during the year after I graduated,[1] and University of Texas at Austin's graduate accounting program is consistently ranked at or near the top in the U.S.[2] I don't say this to brag, but only to state that even with a great accounting foundation I was still the proverbial fish out of water during my first few months in public accounting. There is a certain workplace skill-set which cannot be learned in accounting classrooms, and, for better or for worse, I learned that it is precisely this skill-set that will make or break

---

[1] https://columns.wlu.edu/wl-graduates-secure-highest-pass-rate-of-any-u-s-institution-in-the-cpa-examination/

[2] https://medium.com/texas-mccombs-news/texas-mccombs-accounting-no-1-for-the-10th-year-b9facf2b7027

anyone's experience in public accounting. This is the reason why this book had to be written.

My first assignment on my first day at work was to conduct a financial statement tie out. A financial statement tie out is a review procedure performed just before report issuance to ensure the data in the client's financial statements is clerically accurate and agrees with the data audited by the auditors. Typos, transcription errors, and mistakes can occur whereby an erroneous report is issued—not a great situation. Therefore, a tie out is performed as a final check to ensure the data audited by the audit firm matches the data in the financial statements. Before I began the tie out, a manager spent about ten minutes explaining how to complete the task ahead of me. It was kind of him to do this, but looking back now I probably only understood every third word he said. As a new associate or intern you will quickly find that your firm speaks a proprietary language that was not spoken in your college classes. I nodded along as my manager talked, and he eventually wrapped up his explanation before moving on to another task. I then began the tie out, and the day turned into a total dumpster fire. A task that should have normally taken around two to three hours to complete took almost twelve. After I "completed" it, I took my work to the senior on the job to "go through it" it with her. We spent the next two hours together "going though it" (read "re-doing it"). Fortunately, I kept a humble demeanor throughout our meeting. I think she at least appreciated my mental posture (no one likes a cocksure new hire). At the end of our meeting, I thanked her profusely for "going through it" with me and apologized several times for taking up so much of her time. She then told me something that I will never forget. She said in what could not have been a more matter-of-fact tone, "Thomas, you are new. Everyone at the firm is going to assume you suck for your first six months." In my mind that statement crystallized how new hires are viewed by their more experienced coworkers. Her statement provided a beacon or data point that I could use to chart and adjust my behavior until I gained more experience. Over the next few months it became clear that what she told me could not have been more accurate. As a newly minted graduate on your first day at work you may not feel like you are ready for a promotion, but you also probably will not feel as if you will totally "suck for the next six months." However, unless you are some sort of accounting savant, as a new hire you probably will suck compared to the average associate who has been at your firm for a year or longer. The quicker you internalize this fact the better.

I do not want to sound pessimistic, but I hope that you will grasp this before getting hit in the face with the cold hard truth on the job. Think about your job as a game that everyone else has been playing for many years. You have heard about the game in school but have never actually played it. You do not know the game's lingo, the pieces, or really what it means to "win" the game. Everyone else at your firm does. But in time you will learn how the game is played, and my hope is that this book will accelerate your learning process.

I divided this book into four distinct sections. The first section consists of a short overview of a typical firm hierarchy. Understanding the roles and responsibilities in this hierarchy will be critical to your success at work. The second section is purely devoted to workplace interpersonal skills. The third section covers a few life shortcuts, cheat codes, and some career advice which you can use to find the fast track to success during your first year in public accounting and as you progress in your career. I conclude with a fourth section that contains a real world accounting glossary which includes the accounting lingo you will likely hear at work but probably never heard in the classroom.

"WE ASSUME YOU SUCK"

These words, phrases, and abbreviations are not hard to understand once their meanings have been explained, but many of these terms threw me for a loop as I began my career.

SECTION 1:

FIRM HIERARCHY

CHAPTER 2

YOUR FIRM'S HIERARCHY

As a new audit intern the various job titles at my firm and the responsibilities of each title totally confused me. Without an understanding of the layout of my firm's hierarchy, it was difficult to know which role reported to which and to understand the responsibilities of each position. Whenever I asked a question I was not sure if I was even talking to the right coworker. Sometimes I wondered if there were other job titles at my firm that I didn't know. I have found that many new hires experience the same initial confusion, so I have written this chapter to lay out the typical structure and job responsibilities at a standard accounting firm. While your firm may not be structured exactly as I describe in Figure 2.1, it is probably very similar. I have never heard of an accounting firm that did not have the standard pyramid structure. As you dive into your first few weeks on the job, it is critical that you understand the general layout of the pyramid and the typical job responsibilities of each level within the pyramid.

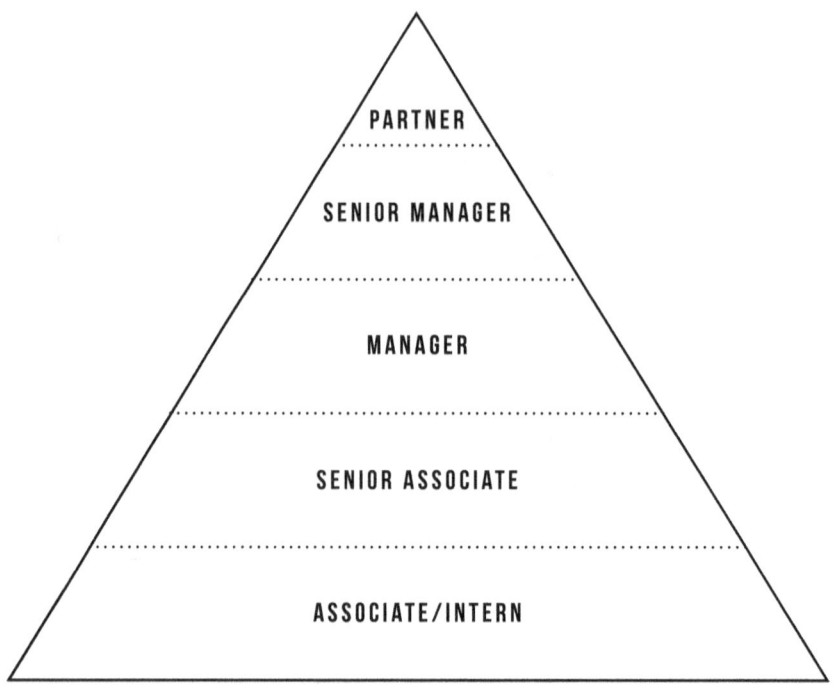

Figure 2.1: Typical Accounting Firm Structure

The bottom level of the firm pyramid is the associate or intern level. This is where most new hires will begin their careers if they have little to no real world accounting experience. Associates, otherwise known as "staff," perform a majority of the less complicated and technical procedures on each engagement. They handle most of the grunt work of any project and will be deep in the details of the project's testing, analysis, research, and procedures. Associates will typically directly report to senior associates or managers. Most firms will ask associates to conduct the same standard testing, procedures, and analysis on each engagement. This type of work is what I like to call the basic blocking and tackling of your practice group. The basics will differ by practice group, but they should be fairly similar from firm to firm. For example, audit associates at all audit firms will probably be asked to conduct the same types of audit procedures over client cash balances. However, the procedures an audit associate at your firm conducts will probably be very different than the research a tax associate conducts, since the end goal of a tax engagement differs from the end goal of an audit engagement. By the end of your time as an associate, you should be able to handle all of the basics of your practice group with ease. If you are given the opportunity to work on a project that is considered to be more complicated than typical associate or intern level work at your firm, recognize that your firm is giving you an opportunity to show that you are ready for a jump to the next level.

The second level of the pyramid is the senior associate level. Senior associates are typically referred to as "seniors" around the accounting industry. It typically takes associates two to three years to receive the promotion to senior. Make it your goal to show that you are ready for promotion to senior associate in the amount of time it normally takes to promote at your firm. If you do a great job during your time as an associate, your firm will most likely promote you. If you are a top performer then it is in your firm's best interest to promote you as your firm will risk losing a trusted (hopefully) member of the team to another employer if you don't "get the nod." Seniors are typically responsible for reviewing the work of associates and/or performing the same blocking and tackling as associates, conducting the more technical testing, procedures, research, and analysis on their engagements, and generally quarterbacking their engagements to ensure they progress smoothly. Seniors typically work the longest hours and are the most stressed of anyone on their engagement teams. At the end of the day the weight of a project usually falls on the senior's shoulders. Most associates and interns are not seasoned enough to be fully relied upon, and managers can always place responsibility (or blame) at the feet of seniors. I could not find any statistics on this, but I would bet the majority of the people who enter public accounting do not make it past the senior associate level. Other job offers can become too good to refuse at the senior level—the world-famous stress of public accounting can take its toll. After the promotion to senior, it normally takes another three years to make the jump to the next level, manager.

Almost all firms want to see five years of experience before promoting a senior associate to manager. Unsurprisingly, managers are responsible for "managing" the jobs that they are assigned. At accounting firms with small clients, managers might be assigned to engagements related to multiple clients at any point in time. Keeping multiple client relationships warm concurrently is a delicate juggling act and a major responsibility for many managers at smaller firms. At firms with larger clients, managers may only be responsible for managing one client or even one area of the engagement. Managers are responsible for reviewing staff and senior work, conducting complicated testing, procedures, research, and analysis, and preparing engagement documentation for review by the engagement Partner. The pressure to recruit new clients begins to increase at the manager level too. The promotion to senior manager and Partner depends upon business development—a Partner's salary is usually proportionate to his book of business. Managers are typically promoted to senior manager after two to four years of manager experience.

Senior managers possess many of the same job responsibilities as managers. As they develop and refine their technical expertise, many senior managers will begin to hone in on a niche practice area (e.g., EBP audits, healthcare deal advisory, airline taxation) to focus on throughout the rest of their careers. The pressure to network and win new clients ramps up to an even greater degree at the senior manager level. As the final promotion is to Partner and a possible ownership stake in the firm, any senior manager up for Partner promotion needs to bring a revenue stream to the firm or at least show she possesses the potential to do so once promoted to Partner.

I have purposefully capitalized the word "Partner" throughout this book to emphasize the fact that you ultimately want to aim for this position. Partners are responsible for building and maintaining books of business and are the ultimate technical resource at their firms. Partner salaries are often determined by the amount they bill each year. Partners typically have an ownership stake in their accounting firms, so they are often both the bosses at the top of the management food chain as well as the owners of their firms. This is why senior managers usually have to bring in a few clients before making Partner or are expected to bring in business soon after making Partner. In addition to the rewards that accompany ownership of their firms, Partners bear the ultimate responsibility for the work performed by their firms. If you are in public accounting you might as well aim to one day be at the top of the profession. My hope is that the remainder of the book puts you on the inside track to do so and clarifies the target in your mind.

SECTION 2:

INTERPERSONAL SKILLS

CHAPTER 3

THE FIRST IMPRESSION

Many people think accounting only involves calculators, taxes, debits, and credits, so you might be asking yourself why we are covering the soft skills subject of interpersonal relations so early on in the book. The fact is that your interpersonal skills will be the dominant determinant of the amount of success you experience during your first year in public accounting. In the longer term, your soft skills will be the most important factor in your career success equation. Your interpersonal skills and emotional intelligence will be the greatest factors your managers and coworkers consider when you are up for promotion. To be frank, as a new hire you will want to possess great people skills and horrendous technical skills over great technical skills and poor people skills. More than anything, you need to be *likeable*. The simple truth is that your coworkers will determine the success you experience as an associate or intern in public accounting. Coworker reviews will determine whether you receive a promotion, get a pay raise, or are offered a position on the team that you want to join. As a new associate or intern you will probably not be asked to complete any highly technical work anyway, and what there is to be done can be taught to you on the job. People skills, on the other hand, are going to be required of you every day at work. You will be faced with difficult clients, annoying coworkers, stressful engagements, and demanding managers. Your people skills will determine whether you successfully move past these obstacles or not. So we must begin with a deep dive into these skills before we proceed with anything else. And before we dive into interpersonal skills we have to start with the cornerstone of likeability: the first impression.

When I was a graduate student at UT Austin, a wise finance professor told our class that once we graduated and entered the working world we should do everything possible to exceed expectations during our first year at work. He said the first impressions and perceptions formed of us by our bosses and coworkers would set the tone for our entire employment, and that once an impression is formed by coworkers it is almost (but not completely) impossible to change it. This statement aligned with my views on human nature, so I made sure to give 100 percent during my first year as an associate. Once I was in the workforce I quickly learned that his advice could not have been more on target. Obviously it is best to give 100 percent effort at all times, but you definitely want to ensure you are going the extra mile during your first year at any job.

Without going too deep into human psychology, most people like to put others into mental boxes that define them completely. A coworker might be "the last one to work every day" or "the first one here." The summer intern might be "lazy" or "a hard worker." A new hire might be "coachable" or "a know-it-all." The first impression you make determines which box you are put in, and it is almost impossible to be moved from the "worse" box to the "better" box. It is much easier to be mentally moved from the "better" box to the "worse" box—a reputation that took years to build can be destroyed through one bad decision. The most important fact about personal qualities is that it does not matter which ones you think you possess—the only ones that matter are the ones your coworkers give you. As you begin your career your goal should be to ensure that you are initially put into the "better" box by your coworkers, and the most effective way to do it is by giving them a fantastic first impression. Your first impression will be the dominant factor by which another person perceives you from your introduction onward. You might be wondering how you can make a fantastic first impression when you have zero experience as a new member of the workforce. Fortunately, you're not expected to have the expertise of a Partner as a new associate or intern. Showing up, having a positive attitude, and showing a willingness to learn—something you clearly already possess because you bought this book—are traits that all firms are looking for in their new hires. Any new hire can bring these traits to the table while possessing zero technical expertise.

You will often see the term "Trial Phase" throughout the remainder of this book. Your Trial Phase is the period of time it takes you to make a great first impression and work your way into your coworkers' good graces. This may take two weeks, six months, or even a year. It will vary by firm and personality type. How you perform during your Trial Phase will make or break your time with your firm. If you have ever been a member of an athletic team, Greek organization, or even a certain friend group, you probably know that nine times out of ten the existing group members want to put newcomers through a test period to determine whether or not the new person is a fit for the group. Most people want to feel like they went through a testing period to join the group they identify with because it gives the group more meaning, so the newcomer must go through a trial period to join the team the same way the existing group members did. Whether existing group members actually went through a testing period is inconsequential. Members of established teams do not gel well with the new guy who, on his first day, acts as if he is already best friends with everyone on the team. The Navy SEALs put new recruits through their legendary Hell Week, most friend groups will not accept the new kid at school until he has proven himself worthy, and public accounting firms are no different. Accept this testing period phenomenon as a fact and use it to your advantage.

You should note that your superiors at your firm are watching to see if you pass your Trial Phase before they see you as a member of the "in" group at work. Membership in the "in" group is not like a junior high clique. It only means being thought of as a person who established coworkers want to work with. These established members of your firm want to be fully confident that they can trust you and that their work experience with you will be positive. It is important to refrain from acting like you are already "in" with your superiors until you are sure that you have passed your Trial Phase, whatever that might look like at your firm. Your firm's Trial Phase will probably consist of putting in a couple months of hard work, making a solid first impression, and not annoying your coworkers. This is all it should take for you to slide into your firm's good graces.

Once you have successfully passed your Trial Phase and people around your office perceive you as being a superstar member of your firm (or even just a slightly above average, B+ member), you will have bought yourself goodwill and a cushion which will be helpful to have in the future. For example, let us suppose you are a little over a year into

THE FIRST IMPRESSION

your career and you sleep through your alarm clock on a Friday morning. You arrive at 10:30 am, even though your firm has an unspoken or even explicit office policy which mandates that associates be at work by 9:00 am. If you have a great workplace reputation with your coworkers because you made great first impressions during your Trial Phase, your coworkers probably will not hold your late arrival against you in their minds. It will be a one-off, freak occurrence that isn't like you. The late arrival will probably be forgotten by lunchtime of that same day. If, on the contrary, you have developed a poor reputation around your office because you made sub-par first impressions during your Trial Phase, the late arrival will be used as another tally against you and will linger in your coworkers' minds indefinitely. There's a great quote in *Hamlet* that reads, "for there is nothing either good or bad, but thinking makes it so."[3] Your late arrival will be considered good or bad depending on which mental boxes you have been placed in by your coworkers. Their perceptions of you from the results of your Trial Phase will be the chief factors that determine how your actions are mentally labeled by them. There are thousands of other scenarios similar to the one described above in which the goodwill bought from the successful completion of your Trial Phase will come in handy. Hopefully now it is easy to see the reasons why you need to set a great tone early.

    In Chapters 4 and 5 I list the best and worst personal qualities to see in new hires as well as the intern and associate scenarios that could put you in one mental box or the other. Try to keep these attributes in mind as you read through the rest of the book and think about how the future choices you make and actions you take could result in you being labeled in your coworkers' minds with these attributes.

---

[3]   Shakespeare, William. *Hamlet*, Act II, Scene II.

CHAPTER 4

ATTRIBUTES OF GREAT ASSOCIATES

I'd like to begin this chapter with a disclaimer: in many of the examples below, I use phrases such as "you want to be viewed as diligent by your coworkers" or "you want to be put in the diligent mental box by your coworkers" rather than "you need to be diligent." I do not use these phrases in an attempt to persuade you to deceive your coworkers by being shallow, surface-level, and only concerned about your outward image. I am rather emphasizing the point that you can be the most diligent advisory associate in America, but if your coworkers do not view you as diligent, then your diligence is for naught in terms of supporting the argument for your promotion and advancement within your firm. You must be diligent *and* be viewed as diligent by your coworkers. I have seen too many examples in which an associate would consider himself diligent—and he may in fact be correct—but his coworkers would not agree for one reason or another. This unspoken discord can last for many months. Eventually at feedback time, unfortunately, the situation will be brought to a head and the associate will be hit with the earth-shattering news that his "diligence" did not do him any good.

Your coworkers will pick up on your attributes in direct and indirect ways. However, they are more likely to believe positive things about you if they see it with their own eyes or hear about it from a third-party rather than from you directly. There are many ways for them to pick up on your attributes indirectly (and they will be looking). Reviewing your work-product, seeing your attitude at work, or hearing about another coworker's experience working with you are just a few ways that perceptions of you will begin to take shape.

Below are the eight major groups of attributes you need to possess as a new hire in public accounting. These are the mental boxes you want to be included within in your coworkers' minds. The reasons why firms are looking for associates and interns with these qualities should be self-explanatory. Rather than go into the obvious reasons why you should strive for these attributes, underneath each one I have listed practical, real life ways for you to display these attributes at work. These actions are just the tip of the iceberg. There are many ways to show that you possess each of these qualities. The scenarios and examples listed below are just to get your mind thinking about the additional steps you can take to show that you possess the attributes of a successful associate or intern.

MENTAL BOXES YOU WANT TO BE IN

(Remember: Whether You Think You Possess These Characteristics Does Not Matter—Only Your Coworkers' Opinions Matter)

ATTRIBUTES OF GREAT ASSOCIATES

1. High Energy, Enthusiastic, and Possessing a Positive Attitude

There is nothing more valuable than bringing positive energy to an accounting firm. As simple and easy as it may seem to show up with great energy and a positive attitude, very few people can bring these attributes to the workplace for extended periods of time. Whether you voted for or against President Trump, his branding of "Low Energy Jeb Bush" and "Sleepy Joe Biden" totally resonated with millions of Americans. In politics and in the workplace, high energy people are often viewed as industrious winners, regardless of how successful they really are. By contrast, low energy people are typically viewed as lazy losers, even if the low energy individuals only suffer from reduced energy levels and not necessarily a lack of success. In addition to making others attracted to you, your coworkers will feed off your great energy, rather than be brought down by your negative or low energy, and your firm will operate with more efficiency.

If you are ever asked, "How are you doing this morning?" by a coworker, do NOT respond with defeated answers like, "Oh, I'm just hanging in there," "It's just another day at the office," or "I'm just trying to make it to five o'clock." These are selfish, negative, pity party answers that will bring you and your coworkers down and turn your coworkers off. Instead, respond to these questions with something along the lines of "You know, I'm having a fantastic morning," "I'm feeling amazing today," or "I got an incredible night's sleep last night and really feel great about today." Find something good about your life and put the focus of your answer on it. Balance and truthfulness are obviously important here. After you respond with a positive answer, watch how the vibe in your office changes for the better. You want your coworkers to know that you are happy to be there and are ready to do whatever it takes to knock out the engagement. However, you do not want to come off as such a high energy person that you are viewed as annoying or cocky by your coworkers. If you are worried that you might have come off too strong with the positivity, throw out a self-deprecating joke when the time is right to strike the correct balance.

Before you head out for the weekend after your first week of work, ask your senior if there is anything you can do over the weekend to get a jump start on the next week's to-do list. After you are comfortable with the basics at work, volunteer for as many tasks as you think you can handle without overburdening yourself. Volunteer for the project no one else wants to work on, especially if it is easy but will only be a time-suck. The possibilities to put forth extra energy at your firm are probably endless—there is always more work to be completed in public accounting. However, do not volunteer for so many tasks that you become unable to see a distinctly laborious assignment through to completion. To use an example from Aesop's fable of "The Tortoise and the Hare," you would like to be viewed as having the best attributes of both animals: the hare's ability to run at a rapid pace toward the goal as well as the tortoise's dogged determination and never quit attitude.

Another way to display positive energy is through your body language. The older I become the more I believe that most communication is non-verbal. Even though your coworkers may not consciously realize it, they will be forming perceptions of you based on your body language from the day they first meet you. When seated at your desk, do not hunch over in a stressed, loser-like position. Keep your hands off your face and out of your hair. Consider the body movements you would make if you were worn-out, anxious, and angry—and do the opposite. Roll your shoulders back while working at your desk and sit up straight. You want to constantly look like you are excited about your work and giving it your best. When walking around the office or at the coffee machine, stand up straight. Don't move around your office hunched over like a hermit. Try to hone in on displaying positive body language before your first day at work when you will be introduced to many of your coworkers for the first time, since the perceptions formed from these initial encounters will be the foundation on which all future opinions of you will be built.

Lastly, remember that no one at work wants to hear about your problems. Your coworkers definitely do not come into work each morning to listen to the personal problems in your life. This is especially true when you are an intern or associate and at the bottom of the firm food chain. Do not be a drain on the team by constantly whining about the difficulties in your life. There is a big difference between a light self-deprecating joke and the public broadcast of a serious problem or personal flaw. Everyone has serious problems and flaws. Keep yours to yourself, find the best solutions to them on your own time, and keep your attention on the job at hand. By talking about your serious problems you might inadvertently expose personal weaknesses that you do not want advertised to your coworkers. In short, you gain nothing by whining about your problems, failures, and shortcomings, but you risk a large downside by exposing them to your coworkers. The negativity associated with your problems will only bring the office down and detract from your reputation of being a high energy and enthusiastic person.

2. Trustworthy and Reliable

Reliability is one of the easiest attributes to display. Showing up on time, keeping your word, communicating, and giving a solid effort is all that is necessary to prove your reliability.

LEAPFROG PUBLIC ACCOUNTING'S LEARNING CURVE

Each evening ask about the timing of when your team plans to arrive at work the next morning. Show up at work on time each morning—or, preferably, earlier than the rest of your team. Those who arrive after you will not know exactly how much of a head start you have on them. By arriving ahead of your team and setting up shop ahead of everyone else, you will be prepared to quickly jump on any early requests made by your seniors and managers as they arrive. If you are going to be late or have to miss work for an unforeseen reason, text or email your team to let them know as early as possible. Nothing is worse than your senior not knowing where you are or when you will arrive. You do not want that uncertainty marinating in your coworkers' minds for any amount of time. You will probably need to take your computer everywhere you travel. If you are working on a special project such as an inventory count, do not forget to bring anything extra needed to complete the task such as count sheets and copies of the selections you have already made. Carry all necessary work gear in a professional backpack or briefcase. Toting a raggedy backpack from college could appear sloppy and unprofessional.

As the new intern or associate on an engagement team you will probably be asked where your team should go for lunch or order take-out from for dinner. Everyone has already been to the spots the old members of the team prefer, so often the new hire gets to make the decision so the team can try something new. Always choose a restaurant that you can completely rely upon to offer a solid meal and a wide variety of options. Everyone should be able to find something on the menu that is desirable. Do not go to your favorite dive bar and grill that serves great burgers only some of the time. There is nothing more unsettling than the new person taking the rest of the members of the team to a lousy restaurant. Put your team ahead of yourself when making this decision. For example, do not take your team to a steakhouse if you have a vegetarian on your team. A bad restaurant will ruin the rest of the day for your team members, and, to make matters even worse, they might subconsciously move closer to thinking that you cannot be trusted to make good decisions.

A sick day early on in your career will appear highly suspicious and your firm's perception of your reliability and commitment to the firm could be brought into question. If you are just feeling tired or hungover, try your hardest to make it to the office and tough it out for the day. However, if you have a serious disease or are contagious, it would not be good for your firm's bottom line if your illness spread amongst the rest of your firm. In this case it would be best for you and your firm if you stay home. If I ever begin to feel like I have a cold coming on or just generally run-down, I take olive leaf extract. I like vitamin C booster pills, but I have found that nothing boosts my immune system quite as well as olive leaf extract. A pill version can usually be found at most grocery stores. I do not have any allergies and am not a physician, so I recommend talking to your doctor about taking it before doing so. It usually takes twelve to twenty-four hours for me to begin to feel the effects of taking it, so I like to take a pill in the evening to give it time to kick in before work the next morning. Also, many new hires in public accounting are fresh out of college and still in party mode. If you think you may have had too much to drink one night, take a daily multi-vitamin (if approved by your doctor) and have a glass of water with a bite to eat before going to sleep. You will wake up feeling much closer to 100 percent than if you went to sleep without these hangover destroyers. Taking little to no sick time off during your Trial Phase will definitely boost the perception of how committed you are to your firm.

Take care to avoid saying anything you could later regret in front of a client. Your firm needs to be able to rely on you to maintain friendly but professional relationships with its clients. The biggest mistake an associate or intern can make is to ruin a firm relationship with a client, so your firm might take precautions. Some firms do not even let their new associates and interns email clients without permission. Do not take it personally if this is the case—just keep working hard until you have proven that you can be trusted in communications with clients.

Lastly, if you tell someone your project will be complete by a certain deadline, meet the deadline. If unforeseen hang-ups occur, communicate these hang-ups immediately. Similar to arriving late for work or having to miss work, it is better to over-communicate rather than under-communicate in almost all situations.

3. Respectful, Appreciative, and Easy-Mannered

The investment your firm makes by hiring you will probably produce negative cash flow during the first few months of your employment. Until you move far enough along the new hire learning curve, you will be a net liability to your firm. In addition to being incompetent on your own, you will actually be an even larger drag on your firm as you slow others down when they take time to show you the ropes. Make sure you show appreciation for the time your firm invests in you. Although it is part of the job for those with experience to teach those without it, taking the time to explain matters to you increases the difficulty of everyone else's job assignments.

My first financial statement audit team included only a manager and me. My manager had been working with this particular client for several years before I was hired and inserted onto the team. He could

ATTRIBUTES OF GREAT ASSOCIATES

have easily completed the job by himself. However, he spent a longer time teaching me the basic blocking and tackling of the audit than it would have taken for him to complete the audit by himself. In the short run, completing the audit by himself would have benefited him and the job budget. However, in the long run I still would not have known what I was doing and would have continued to be a liability to the firm. He sacrificed what could have been a short-term gain for himself for the benefit of the firm and my professional development in the long-term. We ended up developing a great relationship, and he continued to look after me for as long as we worked together. Hopefully you have superiors at your firm who are willing to invest in you like my manager did with me. If a coworker is going the extra mile to show you the ropes, take a moment when it feels appropriate to thank her for the time and energy she has invested into you. Many new hires do not display this respectful and appreciative attitude, so you will stand out among your intern or associate class if you do.

If you are working with one senior or manager in particular on an engagement, check in with him before you leave each evening if you must leave before he leaves. You can say, "Hey, do you think it would be cool if I head out now? I have X, Y, and Z I need to do tonight. I can definitely log back on later tonight if you need me to." If you know in advance that you have to leave early on a certain day, tell your senior as soon as you know. You will learn that some seniors care more than others about associates and interns heading home early, although I believe all care to some extent. You should alter the way you communicate your departure to your senior based on how you think he feels about associates and interns leaving early. It looks much better if you leave early one evening after being the last one on the team out the door each night for the past three weeks than if you leave early on your first day with the team. As an intern I always made sure to check in with my senior before I went home each evening if I had to leave work before my senior left. After several months of this I was told by several seniors that they really appreciated this habit. This is one of the quickest ways to get into their good graces and create goodwill with your coworkers.

When you ride in the same car as a senior, manager, or Partner, let the other person take the front or most desirable seat. You will frequently be sharing rides with coworkers to meet with clients, for meals, and to attend firm events. Nothing looks worse than the new hire taking the best seat in the car.

If you find something wrong with your senior's work, bring it to her attention in the least confrontational manner possible, if it has to be brought up at all. If you can see something is clearly not adding up in another person's work, you can always ask the person to explain the work-paper or document to you. Say, "Hey, I'm running into a wall when trying to make sense of this work-paper. Any chance you can help me understand what is going on here when you have a moment?" Most of the time your senior will catch the mistake when she is explaining the document to you. By phrasing the situation this way you will not directly accuse her of making a mistake and she can give you kudos for having your accounting spidey-senses engaged enough to know that something was not quite right with her work. Try to avoid insulting or indirectly letting someone else think that you believe her work is sub-par. A coworker could take offense, get embarrassed, and may try to throw you under the bus at the next opportunity if she feels like you are attacking her work-product (which her livelihood depends upon).

Maintain respect for your clients at all times, even if they are rude to you or offensive. Public accounting is a client service and client first industry. Your firm's clients ultimately pay your salary and allow you to live a comfortable life. You have no right to ever be rude to or snap back at a client, even if a client is rude or short with you. Each client is undergoing a painful process by having to work with outside accountants—especially auditors—so do not take any rude or offensive behavior personally. Hopefully you never experience any rude behavior at work, but if you do just accept it as part of the job and do not lose any sleep over it.

When you decide to leave your firm, individually reach out to as many people as you think is appropriate to tell them that you will be moving on, that you have enjoyed working with them, and that you hope to stay in touch. People can be shocked by your departure if it does not come with any forewarning. You should aim to leave on the best terms as possible with your coworkers at every level.

4. Possessing a Diligent Work Ethic

Your superiors want to be assured that you will do everything possible to ensure the work assigned to you is successfully completed in the amount of time allotted. You will probably find the last 10 percent of any project seems to take as long as the first 90 percent. When you encounter the tough last 10 percent, double-down, grit your teeth, strap on your helmet, and get the job 100 percent done. Try to avoid leaving a task for someone else before it is 100 percent complete. If you are forced to leave a task before it is complete, leave as detailed notes and open item lists as possible so whoever picks it up after you knows exactly what needs to be done in order to complete the task.

Every Monday, map out the tasks your firm has asked you to accomplish during the week. If you do not think you will be able to complete all of your assigned tasks during a standard week, try to work later or come to work earlier one day during the week to give yourself extra time. Working a few extra hours never hurt anyone. If you still think it will not be possible to complete your assignments, tell your senior or manager as soon as possible so they have a heads up and can plan accordingly.

Know your firm's billable hours goals for associates and make sure you meet, or hopefully exceed, the goal each year. If you begin your career midway through the year, prorate the target accordingly so you keep up the same pace as everyone else. Your firm makes money through billable hours. It is not fair to the rest of the firm if you do not pull your weight. I once worked with a guy who was widely viewed as a senior associate golden boy at our firm. He had the most billable hours out of any senior or associate, could audit the most complex areas of our most complex clients with ease, and he would practically oversee massive SOX consulting jobs as a senior. His golden boy reputation was built by each of these qualities, but I believe his billable hours totals and his well-known work ethic contributed most heavily. Different members of your firm could have different opinions of your technical skills and your ability to work well with others, as these may vary by engagement, but billable hours provide little room for any gray area. They will be an objective piece of evidence supporting your work ethic, so be sure to hit or exceed your firm's hours targets each year.

Make it a point to cut out all distractions at work, especially during your Trial Phase. Don't spend loads of time surfing the web or checking your personal phone while at your desk. In order to be viewed as diligent, your coworkers will need to see you putting forth effort and working hard, not surfing the web or tending to personal matters on your phone. Granted, you may have to take a personal call or use the internet every once in a while, but try to minimize this time and keep it as discreet as possible.

When you have finished a work-paper or another project, take time to do a self-review before signing off on it. Any careless mistake you catch, and thus your reviewer does not, will make your work seem that much more thorough in the eyes of your reviewer and will increase her rating of your work-product. Don't sign off on a work-paper without running a spell check. If I have been battling it out with a work-paper for several hours and finally finish it, I like to step away from my desk, grab a drink of water or a snack, and then return to perform a detailed self-review before signing off. Stepping back, seeing the big picture, and getting your mind out of the weeds can help you see the careless mistakes you made by being engrossed in the details for extended periods of time. Even if you miss something in your testing and your reviewer catches the mistake, producing an organized and clean work-paper that is easy for your reviewer to review will go a long way in building the perception that you can be relied upon to produce a solid work-product.

5. Happy to Be a Team Player

As with any other group, being a team player contributes heavily to your general likeability and is an attribute people are dying to see in any new hire. If you are specifically complimented on something, try to work in a compliment for one of your engagement teammates in your response. If someone says you did a great job on a specific work-paper, respond with something about how you received excellent coaching or help from your senior or manager. Your coworkers will be thrilled when they see you share the glory after a win.

Not calling in sick is another way of being a team player. If you are sick and cannot work, someone else on your team will have to make up for the slack. Remember, your allocated sick days exist for days when you are sick and cannot work. They are not to be viewed as extra vacation days to be taken advantage of each year. Do not burn your employer by using sick days as vacation days. You clearly do not want to come to work if you are contagious, but if you are just feeling tired or hungover you should grind it out and come into the office.

Volunteer for the extra tasks no one wants to do, especially if the tasks are fairly straightforward and easy. You will stand out in other people's minds as someone who sacrificed for the team and your reputation as a team player will grow—even if the work was a breeze and easy for you to complete.

Work within the schedule and framework your senior lays out for you. Do not go solo "hero" mode on a project without asking anyone else on your team which work has the top priority. Your seniors and managers will probably have a master plan in mind on each engagement. As an associate or intern you may not always be privy to the master plan. There will always be a reason why your superiors ask you to complete work in a certain way, so heed their instructions.

Whenever you use your firm's or a client's restroom, wash your hands and leave it in better shape than you found it. If you have not started working full-time yet you might think it is amazing that this has to be said to adults, but you will soon find that some adults can do more damage to a restroom than the most out of control first-grader. You do not want to be the employee who everyone thinks wreaks havoc in the restroom.

If you ever see a piece of trash on the ground at your office or at a client's office, take one for the team, pick it up, and throw it away even if it is not yours. Almost no one in America practices this habit anymore, and you will impress your coworkers and clients by showing that you are not afraid to get your hands dirty for the firm or the client.

6. Competent and Coachable

No one expects you to be a technical accounting expert when you begin your career, but you need to at least have a summary level understanding of the main tasks and issues in your engagements. You should understand the philosophy behind your firm's engagement strategy and the reasons why you need the support your firm has asked you to obtain from your clients. If you do not know something, ask your senior or manager. If you are not asking questions early in your career your superiors will probably assume something is not right instead of assuming that you know what you are doing. Everyone knows what it is like to begin a career in public accounting, so do not be afraid to ask questions.

Whenever new accounting guidance or tax rules are released, try to at least gain a high level understanding of the changes so that you have a cursory understanding of them when your coworkers and clients are talking about them. As a new associate or intern you probably will not be assigned to work on, at least without heavy supervision, any areas under new standards. ASC 606 and ASC 842 were major new standards that were introduced during my years as an audit associate. I would not have considered myself to be an expert on these two new standards then, but I at least knew that our audits could be impacted by the rule changes and knew a general overview of what might trigger a change under the new rules. Only knowing these new standards at a summary level led to dramatically less confusion on my engagements.

You do not have to reach such a level of expertise on the new standards that you could teach a college course on them, but you should at least know the basics to be seen as a competent employee around the office.

If you can become proficient enough in one area of your practice group to give a presentation on it at a firm training, do it. When I was an associate my firm had a senior associate who was widely viewed as an inventory expert at our firm. He gave a professional presentation on inventory counts at a firm training day that was very well received by the rest of our firm. He definitely solidified his reputation as a proficient employee by giving his presentation in front of our entire office. If you could give a similar presentation on any topic related to your job, you would definitely boost your status in the eyes of your firm.

Every work-paper or piece of support will probably have one preparer and at least one reviewer. As the intern or associate on the team, you will always be the preparer. You probably will start to review work prepared by others once you make senior. Obviously you want to aim for as few comments and review notes as possible, but you must realize that you will inevitably receive comments on your work. Do not take any comments or feedback personally or think that your reviewers are leaving comments just to bring you down. Your reviewer might often fix multiple errors and make adjustments that she does not even mention in her work-paper review comments. Comments are meant to be educational or to push the project further towards completion. Your reviewers do not have the time to leave unnecessary comments and feedback. Instead of being upset about a work-paper comment you receive, you should rather be appreciative that your reviewer took the time to bring your mistakes to your attention. I once spent a full week working on a more complicated area of a SOX project. I had some of the basics down but missed many of the details in my testing. After my senior reviewed my work, she sent me a roughly one thousand word essay in an email explaining the details I had missed during the project. She did not have to take the time to do this, but I would have remained unaware and everyone would have been worse off in the long run. It probably took her close to an hour to put the email together, and it was selfless of her to do so. She was viewed as one of our firm's star employees, and this level of care for the job and her coworkers greatly contributed to her reputation. Make sure your coworkers and reviewers know that you welcome and appreciate comments and feedback. It is actually in your best interest to receive as much feedback as possible so you can continue to learn, adapt, and improve. Everyone in public accounting makes mistakes and has weaknesses, just make it a personal goal to daily strengthen your weaknesses and only make the same mistake once.

7. Fantastic Communicator

Communication is simply the transfer of information. On a regular basis, let your engagement team know the status of the work that has been assigned to you. It is far better to over-communicate than under-communicate, especially when the project is not progressing as planned. Although it might feel painful to communicate bad news in the short run, in the long run you will be much better off and thankful you communicated any bad news as soon as you learned about it.

Develop your writing ability and proofread each of your work-papers and emails. Many people think accountants only work with numbers, but in reality you will spend a large chunk of each day drafting emails, writing tick-marks, and documenting your work. Even if math comes easy for you, if you possess poor writing skills you will not get very far in public accounting. Few mistakes reflect more poorly on an associate or intern than a badly written tick-mark or a grammatically inaccurate email sent to a client. If you are worried that your writing ability is at a disastrously low level, it might make sense to download writing software for your computer at work if your firm will give you permission to do so. There is software available for download that will review your writing for grammatical mistakes and will assist you in cleaning up any errors. Another easy way to boost your writing ability is to reread each sentence you type. After rereading a sentence, ask yourself if the sentence would be easily understood in a normal conversation between two parties—if not, rewrite it.

When you are discussing a complicated matter with your coworkers regarding an issue or problem you have encountered, try to explain the situation through a story. As the speaker, it is your responsibility to make it easy for your listener to grasp the crux of the issue, and the most effective way to do this is through a narrative. Human brains are hard-wired to learn through stories. The Bible is one long story, Jesus taught in parables, and when you learned how to add four plus four in elementary school, you probably learned it through a story similar to "John has four apples. Sally gives him four more. How many apples does John have now?" You can probably think of dozens of other problems you have solved by creating back-stories in your mind. In a simple example in which you have run into a problem with a standard accounting procedure and want your senior's approval before proceeding with any further work, you could fill him in on the situation by stating, "I am trying to complete procedure X. I requested invoices in line with our standard testing approach. The client told me the problem is Y though. I am thinking about asking for solution Z now, since this should help us get around Y problem. Does proceeding with solution Z sound OK to you?" By explaining the situation through a narrative your listener has context. The crux of the matter will now be much more clearly defined in his mind than if you had only asked him if proceeding with solution Z would be reasonable without explaining the problem as a whole.

8. Care for Your Work-Product, Your Firm, and Your Firm's Clients

Associates and interns who do not care about their jobs usually do not last long. Just showing that you care about your job and firm will take you much further than you might think. At the end of my second year in public accounting my firm hired a new audit associate straight out of school. He was immediately thrust onto a SOX consulting project, which was probably the toughest way for him to begin his career. I could tell by his body language that his first few days were not going as smoothly as he had hoped, and he was in the middle of a total dogfight with his first engagement. I had briefly introduced myself to him on his first day, but after a few days we had our first real conversation at our firm's weekly Thursday happy hour. He told me he felt like he was moving through the project at a snail's pace, his to-do list seemed to keep growing, and that he was worried the firm might fire him if he didn't turn things around quickly. Of course, unless an extremely grievous non-accounting related infraction is committed, no firm would fire a new hire a week into the job. Everyone in the industry knows new hires experience a major learning curve during their first few months or even years in the industry—which is why I wrote this book. I think deep down my friend thought his job was probably safe for the time being, but I still believed he made the point about being fired only half-jokingly. Regardless, his statements made it obvious that he cared. His mind was definitely in the right place. It was easy to see he was concerned about failing to meet firm expectations and that he cared about delivering a quality work-product. This statement left me with a terrific impression of him, and from that conversation on I wanted him on my engagement team because I knew he cared about the job.

If you are told to work on a project that you think is menial, easy, or elementary, do not complain about the lack of challenging work. More challenging work will come with time. Unless you spend months conducting only mindless work, your career will not suffer for it. During your first few years you need to focus on mastering the basic blocking and tackling of your job. Your firm's expectations of your output and technical expertise will never be lower than during your first year as an associate or intern. Use this time with low expectations to learn as much as possible. There will definitely be something you can learn even in the work you believe is menial. You should enjoy the down time when you get to work on low-stress projects that you can easily handle. Learn something about your coworkers, the client, or the engagement process in the temporarily relaxed environment.

If a stranger or client is waiting awkwardly in your firm's lobby or workspace, introduce yourself to him. Ask if there is anything that you can help him with or anyone who he would like you to take him to see. Many of your coworkers will walk right by the stranger without checking in on him even though awkwardly standing in an unfamiliar office is uncomfortable for everyone. To make matters worse these people typically are your clients or prospective clients. Saying hello and checking in with him will show that you have the personal confidence and initiative to introduce yourself to someone without being prompted—something not everyone possesses—and that you desire to ensure outsiders have a positive experience with your firm. He may even compliment you to your Partner by telling your Partner how hospitable you were to him. Your Partner will be thrilled to hear about you going above and beyond to represent her firm in this hospitable and caring manner.

Always carry a dozen or so business cards in your wallet. Make sure that the cards don't crumple or wear out while lodged in your wallet for extended periods of time. Winning a client as an associate or intern is almost unheard of and would definitely put you on the fast track to success at your firm. Know your firm's specialty practices so you have the ability to provide a one-minute elevator pitch to any potential clients you meet. Your firm's website should have a listing of all its practice areas. You do not have to be an expert in these practices— you just need to be able to give about a one-minute summary of the practice areas to prospects so they can determine if your firm provides the services they need. However, don't make any promises or put your firm on the hook for anything. Your firm's Partners will have to make the final decision over whether your firm brings any prospect on as a client. The best case scenario when prospecting is that you leave each conversation having arranged an introduction between the prospect and one of your firm's Partners. Your firm's Partner group will have to determine if the prospect is the right fit after one of them meets with the prospect. Either way, your Partners will be appreciative and impressed that you presented them with a potential opportunity to win new business.

CHAPTER 5

ATTRIBUTES OF SUBSTANDARD ASSOCIATES

Now that we have discussed the attributes of great associates, I want to contrast the attributes of great associates with the attributes of substandard associates. Remember, it doesn't matter if you think you don't possess any of these attributes. Only your coworkers' opinions and the mental boxes they put you in matter. Underneath each attribute below are a few actions you can take and behaviors you should avoid to limit the chances that you are labeled with any of these attributes. Many additional actions can be taken or avoided to reduce the risk of being put in any of these negative mental boxes, but the practical actions and behavior patterns discussed below should get the ball rolling in your mind.

MENTAL BOXES YOU DON'T WANT TO BE IN

1. Untrustworthy and Unreliable

You don't want to forget about and miss any scheduled meetings or events at work. It's easy to forget about a meeting or phone call that you scheduled weeks in advance. Most firms will provide you with an online calendar that is synched with your email. Whether you receive a firm-issued calendar or not, you should organize all scheduled events in a firm calendar, your own online calendar, or notebook. Put everything in your calendar: phone calls, scheduled client time, meetings, CPA exams, vacation time, and anything else related to work. When you get to work in the mornings and leave for home in the evenings, check your work calendar to look over upcoming events and meetings, especially for the next day and the rest of the week. I cannot tell you how many times doing this quick check has saved me from missing a meeting or from going to the wrong location. Just showing up on time and at the right place is a big part of not being put in the unreliable mental box, so let your work calendar work for you to prevent this from happening.

When asked by a manager how long you estimate it will take you to complete a task, lean toward overestimating rather than underestimating the amount of time you think is necessary. If you say three hours and it only takes you two hours to complete the task, you have over-delivered ahead of schedule. But if you say two hours and it takes you three hours, you are moving behind schedule. Remember, your manager does not know how long it will take you to complete the task. If he did, he would not have asked in the first place. You set his expectations by your response to his initial request for a timetable.

ATTRIBUTES OF SUBSTANDARD ASSOCIATES

Many firms have Work-From-Home (WFH) policies. Even if your firm permits you to work from home on certain days of the week, try to work from your firm's office as much as possible (especially during your Trial Phase). You need to be seen around the office when you are a new hire to build trust and relationships. You do not want to be the employee no one at your firm ever sees. In regards to WFH policies, to be frank, it is best for you to operate under the assumption that whenever you WFH, your coworkers will assume you are not being quite as productive as you would be if you were working from your office. Personally, I will admit that work that takes me eight hours to complete in the office usually takes nine to ten hours to complete if I am at home. Almost everyone I have talked to about this has said the same because deep down almost everyone knows it is true. I actually am starting to think the abbreviation "WFH" was coined because it was too painful for people to spell out in written communication when they were working from their homes. Just writing "WFH" makes the situation seem much more professional and allows the writer to get the embarrassment over with quickly. There might be times when you have to work at home, but as a general rule work from your office as much as you can.

If you are going to be late to work in the morning, text your senior and/or manager to let them know why you are running late and when you expect to arrive. The text will be welcomed by them. They are much more likely to not think twice about your tardiness if you send a text or email in advance. Giving a heads up in advance will show great accountability instead of showing up late unannounced. If you know you need to take vacation or have a personal matter to tend to during the work week, let your firm know about it as far in advance as possible. Try not to drop these events at the last minute and definitely don't wait until after the event has already happened.

2. Disrespectful and No Sense of Place

When you first join your firm you should realize that you are the new hire and you need to pay your dues. You should indirectly let your coworkers know that you recognize your inexperience may be slowing them down and that you appreciate them taking the time to show you the ropes. In addition to displaying a grateful attitude when just beginning your career, do not be afraid to add value to your firm wherever it is possible. If there are odd jobs that you can do around your firm's office such as taking out the trash or running the company dishwasher, do not hesitate to jump on these tasks when the time is right. Your superiors will be impressed when they see you doing whatever you can to pitch in and add value to your firm.

When you are in the Trial Phase you should attempt to steer clear of any arguments or disagreements with your coworkers. This is especially true if you are talking to someone higher up the corporate ladder than you. Even light banter could come across as disrespectful at some level, and you gain nothing by disagreeing with your coworkers. If a coworker attempts to convince you to participate in something illegal, unethical, or immoral, obviously you need to stand your ground. Outside of anything that would compromise your integrity, however, as the new hire your first priority should be to ensure you avoid stepping on any toes. Even if you are arguing over something as light as a sports team, your coworker may be emotionally invested and may not take your disagreement well. People are sometimes seriously emotionally attached to objects, ideas, or theories that others would view as inconsequential (like a sports team), so take care not to get into even playful arguments in your Trial Phase. You don't stand to gain much by arguing, but you risk a massive downside. If someone says something you disagree with, just smile and nod your head rather than present a counterpoint.

If you are ever working while wearing headphones or earbuds and a coworker tries to verbally say something to you, physically remove your earphones to listen to what your coworker has to say. Don't just turn the volume down. Physically removing your headphones shows respect for the person speaking and proves that you are giving 100 percent of your attention to the speaker. You might be seriously trying to listen while turning down the volume, but your coworker cannot see your attempt to listen unless you physically remove your earphones.

If your firm ever puts on a company employee training day, make the most of it. Remember that by hosting a training day your firm is actually paying you to sharpen your accounting skills. Do not squander these opportunities by refusing to give them your full attention. Put your cell phone away and do not use your laptop for anything other than taking notes related to the training. Some Partners may consider the use of your phone or the personal use of your computer during a training session to be disrespectful. You will stand out if you purposefully take an interest in learning from the training by paying attention.

Make a point to be as friendly and warm as possible to your firm's HR, Admin, and Maintenance teams. Your firm could not function without them, and these people have much more clout than some new hires realize. They can make your life at work miserable or like a dream. Some client-facing coworkers may view these employees as support staff whose jobs only exist to make life easier for the client-facing employees. They might even view support staff as lower priority employees and treat them as such. Do not make this massive mistake. Your firm's HR, Admin, and Maintenance teams will definitely be in the ear of your firm's Partners and may in fact be closer to the Partner group than your firm's highest ranking senior manager. Members of these teams will take note if you do not treat them like you would treat anyone else at your firm. Anyone on these teams can make things very difficult for you, so go out of your way to give them as little incentive as possible to do so.

3. Sloppy and Unprofessional

Clean up each of your social media accounts when job searching and/or before you start work. Employers will search for your social media when recruiting you. Even after you are hired, strive to keep all social media as clean as possible. Whenever I heard about a new hire joining my firm (or especially my future engagement team), I would often look the person up on social media to get a gauge on how well we might work together. Your social media may be the basis upon which many future coworkers form their first impressions of you. A large percentage of the firm-wide perception of you could be established before your first day at work, so do not let a silly social media post impact the perception in a negative fashion.

Go to your firm's social events. If your firm's Partners have been nice enough to organize a happy hour or social event, the least you can do is show up. Avoid having more than two drinks when you are out with coworkers (if you have to drink at all). Being the office partier is not the reputation you want to cultivate. You do not want to ruin your reputation at work due to one night with too many beers in front of your coworkers. You have worked too hard in school and hopefully on the job to blow it all on one drunken night. As a side note related to drinking at work events, a good rule of thumb is to put your car keys away for the day whenever you have or expect to have any alcohol.

ATTRIBUTES OF SUBSTANDARD ASSOCIATES

Use a ride-sharing service or catch a ride home with someone else when you drink. Outside of random accidents, illnesses, and mistakes that cannot be prevented, there are three major potential pitfalls in American life that can bring Americans down hard:

1. Drinking and driving: this can lead to car wrecks, mutilations and deaths, lawsuits, DUIs, prison time, and other disasters you want to avoid
2. Dating or marrying the wrong person
3. Drug addictions and drug overdoses

If you can avoid falling into any of these three self-destructive pitfalls, you are probably going to have a fine life. I believe that anyone can bounce back after falling into one of these pitfalls, but by making a decision never to drink and drive again you practically eliminate one of the three pitfalls and give yourself a much better chance to have a successful career and enjoyable life.

Each time you step away from your computer, lock the screen or turn it off. You want to lower the risk of an unauthorized person seeing confidential information on your computer—allowing confidential information to fall into the wrong hands is one of the gravest mistakes you can make in public accounting. If a client sees you leave your computer screen unlocked, she may begin to think your firm does not value the confidentiality of her company's data. You do not want a client to think this, so build a habit of locking your computer each time you step away from it.

Check your language at work. I totally understand that public accounting can be stressful. You may encounter many situations that you think warrant swearing. But you want to come off as a class act to your coworkers, and swearing will not help you in this endeavor. Even if you think a certain word is not necessarily a bad word, your coworkers may consider it impolite. In addition to keeping your language clean around your coworkers, make a point to act the same way in front of clients or in any written messages.

A lack of responsiveness is one of the most common (and valid) complaints clients can have with their external accountants. Personally, I have heard of more people leaving their accountant due to simply a lack of responsiveness than for any other reason. In addition to trusting you to provide exceptional service, clients desire to ensure you have received all their communications and understand their questions and concerns. Make it a rule to return all client calls and emails within 24 hours. If you are going on vacation or are out of the office, set an automatic reply email and voicemail to automatically share your status with clients and/or to redirect their communications to another person at your firm if needed.

You will be writing and reading emails everyday as a public accountant. Every email you send needs to be professional. Use a professional font in black only, unless you wish to emphasize particular words for the benefit of the reader. End every email with a professional closing and signature. Read through each email before you send it to ensure proper spelling and grammar, even if the recipient is a close friend. One of my former coworkers and close friends wrote even casual emails to me in the most professional manner, even when we were sitting right next to each other at our office. I used to give her a hard time for doing this, but this practice was actually a smart move on her part. Remember that any email can be forwarded to anyone else with an email address and will exist for the rest of time. When rereading through your email draft, remember to check the recipient and anyone who is carbon copied for accuracy. Entering the recipient's email address after you have typed your message will prevent you from accidentally sending someone a partially written message. You want to do everything you can to minimize the risk of making a careless mistake, and the odds of you making a careless mistake drop substantially if you will just take a minute to reread each email before letting it fly.

Do not visit any websites on your firm-issued laptop or via your firm's Wi-Fi that could embarrass you if your browsing history was made public. Your firm-issued laptop and your firm's Wi-Fi are your firm's property, so your firm could stumble upon your search history during its routine IT maintenance activities. Your firm also will probably retain the legal right to inspect your search history if it so chooses. Your firm's IT department may even be able to access your browsing history without having physical access to your computer. Some internet content that may seem harmless to you could come across as seriously unprofessional to one of your firm's Partners. Use the internet as conservatively as possible and also keep in mind that nothing you're looking at is private.

Learn your office dress code and wear that level of clothing or higher. Your firm may want you to dress up or down depending on the client you are assigned to work on. You can boost your coworkers' perception of you as being someone who takes the job seriously by dressing like someone who takes the job seriously. You do not have to drive a fancy sports car and wear $1,000 suits into the office each day, but you should not dress like you are still a penniless student. You may not be wealthy, but you are probably making enough to buy a few nice sets of clothes to wear to work.

4. Conceited and Uncoachable

Nobody likes a conceited new intern or associate. There is no reason for a new employee to be cocky on the job. Do not let your head get too big, even if you do receive some positive feedback from your coworkers. You will probably still be a net liability to the firm during your first few months even if you are told you are exceeding expectations. Your coworkers have passed the CPA exams, been through stressful engagements, and signed off on highly complicated, highly technical work-papers. As a brand new associate you will need to earn respect over time.

In addition to receiving feedback on specific projects and work-papers, you want to generate as much feedback as possible on your higher-level habits and tendencies, especially early in your career. Do not get defensive or argue when you receive feedback. It is in your best interest for feedback to be generated so your bad habits and mistakes can be brought to light and corrected sooner rather than later. You should try to keep an on-going personal feedback file in which you keep copies or notes of all feedback, good and bad. Keeping up with this file may be a small pain in the short run, but in the long run you will be much better off and less likely to repeat mistakes. The deliverer of your feedback will be pleased when she sees you making an effort to write her communication to you down. Remember that it is painful and a hassle for your coworkers to give you feedback, so make sure they know that you appreciate them taking the time to show you the ropes.

You will definitely make mistakes at work. When you make one, be the employee who is not afraid to claim responsibility for it. If you are not making mistakes, then you probably are not being pushed as hard as you should be. When you recognize that you have made a mistake, try to fix it quickly and quietly (only if it's legal and ethical to do so). If you think you made a mistake and you don't believe you can fix it by yourself or without additional guidance, go to your manager, lay

ATTRIBUTES OF SUBSTANDARD ASSOCIATES

out the situation succinctly, admit that you may have made a mistake, and let your manager direct your next steps. Your manager will be impressed that you recognized the mistake and were humble enough to bring it to her attention before she found it. She will know that you now know how to avoid the mistake in the future and will probably trust you with more work. Because so few millennials are able to admit mistakes, this is actually one way that you can differentiate yourself from your peers. As long as you're not constantly making mistakes and making the same mistakes over and over again, you will not be dinged for being quick to claim responsibility for a mistake.

5. Unable to Work with Others

During your first year you will constantly be working on tasks under the supervision of a senior or someone higher up the pyramid. In addition to monitoring and supervising your work, your senior will have her own projects and tasks to complete. You will inevitably run into questions and roadblocks while working on your assigned tasks while underneath the supervision of your senior. Once you are put on an engagement team, ask your senior how she would prefer you ask her questions. Some seniors will want you to work for several hours, formulate a list of questions, and then meet together at the end of the day to go over all of your questions in one sitting. This process will allow these seniors to work for extended periods of time on their own projects without interruptions from you. Other seniors may want you to run your questions by them as soon as possible in order to keep the project rolling with as few hiccups as possible. Either way, it will be irritating for your seniors if you do not ask questions in their preferred manner, so always discuss the preferred method beforehand. In my experience, very few people like to be asked a question when they are in the middle of their own project. If you know your senior prefers a list of questions at planned meetings, a great way to set this up is to say "Hey senior, is there any chance that I could run a few things by you whenever you have a moment?" This indirectly lets your senior know that you respect her position and her time but it also gets the point across that you need to circle the wagons with her before you can proceed.

If a coworker ever asks you to send him a certain file, email, or password, send it to him ASAP. Do not wait until you have finished your current project. If you can't send it immediately, let him know the reason why and when he might expect to receive it. He will probably be twiddling his thumbs at his computer waiting to receive what he needs from you. By letting him know the status of the information he needs, you show that you respect his time and ensure your firm operates with maximum efficiency

Your coworkers will make mistakes and disappoint you. You will do the same to them. Give other people the benefit of the doubt when they make mistakes, and they will reciprocate. Do not cast blame or hold grudges against your coworkers. Engaging in this negative behavior will be a distraction and could lead to potential disaster for you, your firm, and your clients. At the end of the day you are all on the same team.

You never want to be the intern or associate who your managers specifically request off their engagement teams. This will create an extra headache for your Partners in their job planning and scheduling, and it will be a poor reflection on you. Instead, you want to be the pleasant and friendly associate who each manager wants on his team. Even if you are not as technically sound as your peers, a manager might still request to have you on his team because you are a pleasant person who is easy to work with. He can teach you anything technical you might need to know for the project, but he will not be able to teach you personal skills and behavior patterns necessary to work well with others.

Try to repeat requests made of you by your managers back to them so they know that you received their requests and grasp what has been asked of you. Always carry a notebook for note taking when directions are verbally given to you. Everyone at your firm will love to see you taking notes, since it implicitly shows you care about what they're telling you and will see to it that the job is done correctly. This act will add to your reputation of being an employee who cares about the job and who others want on their engagement teams.

If you know that you will be working with a specific senior on a project and your office has open seating, you may want to sit next to the senior so the two of you can communicate easily. Sitting nearby will make it easier for your senior to relay instructions to you and easier for you to ask questions and show him problems. You will also come off as someone who takes the job seriously because you are doing the opposite of shirking away or trying to hide from your senior. If you arrive early and stay late, then your senior will not be able to help but notice how diligent and reliable you are. Obviously, if all of your firm's seniors typically sit together then you may not want to charge into the herd of seniors as an associate or intern. However, if employees of all levels have an intermixed seating arrangement, do not hesitate to find a seat next to your senior. If you do not know how to ask questions properly and are annoying your senior with constant interrogatories, sitting next to your senior will work against you. If you can figure out how to walk the line between annoying and not asking enough questions, by the end of an engagement your senior will probably be left with a terrific impression of you.

6. Negative, a Grumbler, and a Complainer

After you make a mistake, take responsibility for it, learn from it so you do not repeat it, handle it gracefully, and then move on. Do not think about your mistakes as your failures. Rather, think about them as personal learning opportunities. Do not moan and groan about your mistakes or try to pass blame onto someone else. More experienced members of your firm will know exactly why your mistakes were made and who made them—they've likely made the same mistakes—so it is not in your best interest to try to blame someone else. Do not go so far as to beat yourself up over a mistake though. Although some self-deprecating jokes can be great, full on self-loathing will never be a good look for you. Nothing good comes from beating yourself up. The most productive people in life realize the past is the past and that it cannot be changed. Focus on the future and don't let a mistake slow you down or lead to more mistakes.

During the beginning of your career your firm may spend a lot of time training you. If a coworker is attempting to explain something to you and you are not getting it, never moan and groan about not understanding the subject matter. Every middle school class has the one kid who complains to the teacher and whines "I don't get it" after the teacher makes each point. You don't want to be this person at work. No one is going to feel sorry for you for not understanding something and no one wants to listen to you throw a pity-party. Respectfully asking your more experienced coworker if he can explain something one more time using the proper tone and posture is totally in-bounds, but no one wants to continue repeating a point to the "I don't get it" employee.

Never write anything in an email, in your office chat messenger, or in an any survey or feedback request that you would not want publicly

ATTRIBUTES OF SUBSTANDARD ASSOCIATES

broadcasted to the rest of your firm. Of course it is a best practice to refrain from saying anything negative about any situation or person, but take special care to avoid writing something that could come back to haunt you down the line. Also, context can easily be lost in any written message. Nothing good can come from a negative message, but there is unlimited downside potential.

Finally, don't complain about long hours, a terrible client, or another coworker, especially in writing. Try to find something to love about your experience and keep pushing. You are not storming Normandy by being in public accounting, and millions if not billions of people around the world would gladly trade their jobs for yours if given the chance.

7. Uninterested in the Success of the Firm

Do not turn down work. Unless you are actually completely swamped, if a manager asks if you can complete something try to make the time for it, especially during your Trial Phase. If there is a time constraint and you are already working on a different project for another manager, tell the second manager that you are already working on something for another manager but can get to the second project as soon as your current project is completed—or now if your current manager approves it. You will look good in the second manager's eyes by telling her that you are already in the midst of working on something. You will be perceived as busy, in demand, and someone who managers trust with work.

Constantly being given new assignments and tasks is a good thing. It shows that your firm trusts you to produce a solid work-product and that your job security is probably stable. You want to be seen as in demand by the rest of your firm. If after a few months of working you find that you are one of the only associates or interns who is rarely assigned work, then you probably should think about scheduling a meeting with one of your higher-ups to discuss the lack of assignments. This meeting would also show your interest in the success of the firm. You probably don't need to worry about a lack of work and its implications unless you have been at your firm for at least a few months. Everyone's first few weeks can be slow since it is often difficult to integrate new hires into existing projects.

Try to develop solutions or plans of action before you bring a question or a problem to a senior. You might say, "I've run into problem X. I was thinking we could do Y to get around it, but I wanted to run this by you first before I risked wasting time doing it that way." This kind of statement lets your senior know that you respect her authority but have also at least thought of possible solutions to the problem at hand. Spinning your wheels on a project is not good for the job budget, so your senior will be pleased that you had the budget in mind as you presented her with the problem and a possible solution.

Instead of seeking to do only the bare minimum, after you have finished your assigned work try to anticipate and act on your team's future needs so that efficiency is maximized. However, I don't suggest doing this until you have been working for a few months and feel comfortable with the engagement process. You don't want to mistakenly spend time working on a task that your team doesn't need you to work on. For example, if you and your manager are working on a project together and he is relying on you to relay certain information to him, try to find the answers to his questions that you can reasonably anticipate ahead of time. Everyone loves the person who can provide an answer to a problem quickly or before the problem even presents itself.

ATTRIBUTES OF SUBSTANDARD ASSOCIATES

Now that we have gone over a few ways that you can avoid falling into the negative mental boxes, we will move on to a few simple ideas to boost your general likeability at any accounting firm.

CHAPTER 6

LIKEABILITY BEST PRACTICES

This likeability chapter is filled with anecdotal advice that I have used to connect with others in the past. Some of it will need to be tailored to your specific situation, but your career should advance by leaps and bounds if you can act on the tips and suggestions below.

Say "hello" or "good morning" to your coworkers and clients when you first see them each morning, and "good-bye" or "have a great night" each evening before you or they head home for the night. Greeting and bidding farewell to the people around you will break the ice each morning and have you heading home on a solid note each evening. Unless your coworkers are arriving late or leaving early, they generally will love to be acknowledged upon their arrivals and departures. Don't force it if it isn't there, but these simple words can be incredibly powerful in addition to being friendly and courteous at face value. If you greet a specific person in front of a crowd, the crowd will pick up on the fact that you are confident enough to say hello, which not everyone can do. On top of this, a perception of you as a pleasant and well-liked person will probably begin to be formed by the group.

If a coworker has gone the extra mile for you, you may want to give him a Christmas present (or a thank you present anytime during the year) to thank him for the extra time and energy he invested in you. As a new associate I had a senior who went out of his way for me frequently during my first year. The icing on the cake was when he invited me over for one of his famous "king's breakfasts" at his home one December morning before we departed on a road trip to a client site. He put me in charge of cooking the bacon, and I unfortunately burned it to a black crisp while he was out of the room. I felt bad about this since he and I were just getting to know each other. A couple of days later I realized that Christmas was only a few weeks away. It presented me with the perfect opportunity to send him a gift to make up for the burned bacon and show my gratitude for his generosity and guidance during my first year. My college roommate's mom gave my roommates and me a breakfast sandwich maker during my senior year of college. I was able to quickly put together hundreds of delicious sausage, egg, and cheese breakfast sandwiches on that machine during my senior year (thank you, Mrs. Olson). I decided the breakfast sandwich maker would be the perfect peace offering for the burned bacon while also functioning as a Christmas present/thank you for looking out for me and showing me the ropes during my first year. The $25 I spent on the gift was nothing compared to the goodwill it bought me. I had it shipped to my senior's home address in Christmas wrapping paper. After he received it he told me he was totally blown away by the gift, and our friendship was that much stronger for it.

LIKEABILITY BEST PRACTICES

People want to work with the people they enjoy being with. You should make a concerted effort to get to know your coworkers as soon as you can. Don't act like you're best friends with everyone at your firm right off the bat though. Try to become true friends with your coworkers, even if making friends is hard for you. I understand many accountants have a hard time making friends, but if you want to be successful in public accounting it is vital that you make friends at your firm. One way to make friends is to ask your coworkers about their lives. Make it a goal to ask three questions (without being an annoyance) for every statement you make about yourself. It's a fact of life that human beings love to talk about themselves. It just makes people feel good. By asking questions about your coworkers' lives you will subconsciously stand out as someone who makes them feel good even though they do most of the talking during your conversations. You never want to ask about anything too personal, so try to keep your conversations light and loose. The following are questions you can ask any of your coworkers regardless of how well you know them:

- "Did you do anything fun last night after work?"
- "What do you have going on for/what did you bring for lunch today?" (Some people think lunch is the most exciting part of each day.)
- "Do you have any big plans this weekend?"

After you ask these questions, try to remember the responses you receive. You will stand out if you ask how your coworker enjoyed the event, meal, weekend, etc. after the fact. Asking about the event afterward proves you actually listened. The answers to these questions will also give you great material to ask follow up questions in order to keep the conversational ball rolling. If your coworker (or anyone in life for that matter) ever asks you a question, the least you can do is ask her the same question in return after you give her your response. I am blown away by the pathetic conversational skills of so many people who can't get this elementary piece of conversational etiquette down. If a coworker asks about what you did over the previous weekend, tell her, and then ask her about her weekend in return at a minimum. Don't tell her how yours was and then wait for her to ask another question or make another statement. Treat the conversation like a ping-pong game or tennis match. If you do not ask a question in return, it is analogous to her hitting the ball to you in anticipation of rallying with you, without you hitting the ball back to her. By asking her a question in return you hit the ball and keep the rally alive. If you're not very responsive, she will probably begin to feel less inclined to talk with you. Hopefully it's easy to see how important it is to hit the ball back and at a minimum ask her the same question in response.

Unless eating out for lunch compromises your budget, go out with coworkers as much as you can. Eating lunch with your colleagues provides you with a fantastic opportunity to develop relationships. The value of the few extra dollars you spend eating out will be minuscule in comparison to the value of the relationships you develop. If there is a crew in your office who consistently goes out for lunch, you may not be invited to eat out with them until you've been there a few months. This may be a standard part of the Trial Phase and is to be expected. Wait for them to invite you and seize the opportunity when it comes. If you decide to bring your lunch to work and eat at your desk, show consideration for your coworkers by being mindful of the way your food smells and your eating habits. You don't want to be the new hire who brings a smelly meal to work and fills the entire office with a foul smell.

If you are on good terms with a coworker and know he is either married or in a relationship, asking him about how he met his significant other can be a terrific question to get him talking. Everyone loves to talk about significant others. I don't recommend asking this in an introductory conversation, only if you have already had a few good conversations with the person and can work the topic in smoothly. Your coworker will definitely feel more connected with you after telling you about the people he deeply cares about.

If you believe that you are not great at connecting with people (and many accountants are not), you might try finding things to like about your coworkers and mirroring their communication styles in order to drum up a connection with them. If I find things to like about people (even without telling them) they will somehow always pick up on it and begin to like me more as a direct result of me finding things to like about them. I am convinced this phenomenon has to be the result of a subconscious communication transmitted via body language or tone of voice—remember that a majority of communication is non-verbal—that the other person's subconscious senses. Mirroring another person's communication style can draw the person to you as well. If the person you are speaking with talks in an upbeat, energetic tone or tempo, you should try to match it. If he uses unique words or phrases, you should use those same words and phrases. If he speaks at a low volume, you should speak at a low volume. If he likes to keep his distance physically when speaking, you should make sure you keep an adequate distance. People connect with those who are most like them, and the subconscious can pick up on even the tiniest signals from others without the conscious realizing what is happening. For example, when one person yawns, often everyone else in the room will yawn without consciously deciding to yawn. There is clearly something going on at a subconscious level between those in conversation, so use mirroring to your advantage. Find things to like about your coworkers and mirror their actions, and they will begin to show signs of total connection with you.

Many companies now organize office fantasy sports leagues. Even if you don't follow sports, play in these leagues. Participating gives you an opportunity to get to know your coworkers and gives you another perfectly acceptable and easy topic to talk about within your office. I didn't play in my office leagues during my first year as an associate and definitely missed out. If you happen to win a league or a week, try to handle it with grace. Avoid boasting or coming off as overexcited about your win. Your coworkers will probably be turned off by poor sportsmanship, and nothing is cooler than a person who can win big and act like the win is not a big deal.

Take time to introduce yourself to the new employee at your firm when you see him on his first day. Every new hire is eager for someone to come along and ease the tension of a first day at work. If you are not exactly sure about what to say, you can always say something like, "Hey, my name is Thomas. I don't think we've met yet. I'm in the tax practice here. How has the first day/week gone for you?" Any new employee will be incredibly grateful that you took the time to introduce yourself, and you will gain an instant friend by doing so.

If you park your car in your firm parking lot, make sure you park it between the lines in a designated parking spot (especially if your lot is crowded). Your coworkers will eventually figure out which car is yours. You never want to take up two of your firm's parking spots due to a poor parking job. None of your car's tires should be touching the lines outlining your parking spot. If a coworker has to park farther away from your office thanks to you, you could easily draw her ire (especially if she is in a rush, late to a meeting, or just not in a good mood).

Arriving earlier and staying later than your coworkers in your Trial Phase is so critical that it warrants a final paragraph to emphasize the point. Your arrival and departure times at work each day will probably be the number one data point most of your coworkers initially use to form their perceptions of you. They will be so obvious and say so much about you that your coworkers will not be able to help but use the timing of your comings and goings as the chief factor they consider when sizing you up. If you like to study for the CPA early in the morning before work or late at night after work, try to study from the office instead of at home. Even if your coworkers know you are only studying for the CPA, the physical sight of you at the office early in the morning and/or late at night will give all of your coworkers a terrific impression of you. When working with a particular senior, at a minimum aim to arrive as early and stay as late as your senior, unless you have a legitimate reason for not doing so. Even if you do not act on any of my other advice but do follow through with arriving early and staying late, then this action of and by itself will be enough to set you up for a fantastic start to your career.

CHAPTER 7

HOW TO TALK TO CLIENTS AND COWORKERS

To conclude this section on interpersonal skills, I want to discuss how to best communicate with clients and coworkers. The masses could not be more mistaken in their jokes about accountants having no people skills. An enormous part of experiencing success in public accounting is creating friendly but professional and independent relationships with your firm's clients. Some public accounting services may require the most delicate sales job out there. For example, auditors sell services that actually inflict pain on their clients. Outside of the medical field, I have not heard of any other industry like this. No matter which practice group you join, it is not going to be fun for your clients to be poked and prodded by you. Below are some general conversational topics that are in-bounds and some that are out-of-bounds for discussion with your clients and coworkers.

Topics that are in-bounds for discussion:

- The events of the previous night, previous weekend, or the upcoming weekend (make sure you keep it clean)
- Food or meals
- Positive attributes of your coworkers and client team members
- Sports teams and games
- Major (non-political) current events
- Music tastes
- Hobbies

Topics that are out-of-bounds for discussion:

- Political views
- Your sex life
- Any drug use or excessive alcohol consumption
- Negative attributes of your coworkers or clients
- How sure you are that you will be promoted or the positive feedback you received

With these broad conversational topics in mind, the general tips and tricks below should be of assistance when navigating the waters of conversation with clients and coworkers:

If you find an error on the client's part, the person responsible will look incompetent in front of his superior. Whether you are dealing with an AR clerk or the CFO, keep in mind that each is worried you might find a mistake (or fraudulent activity) he was responsible for and embarrass him in front of his boss.

Fraud is very serious in the business world. It would be better for any job applicant in America to write the other f-word on a job application than to disclose anything related to his involvement with fraud.

You should never throw the word "fraud" around lightly in your office. Don't even think about talking about it loosely at a client site. If your team does find evidence of fraud, it is best to let your manager or Partner discuss it with the client before you bring it up.

You will often participate in conference calls as an associate or intern. If you are leading the call, as soon as you are connected to the group state your name and the names of the other people in the room who are on the call with you. This is common conference call courtesy. If leading the call, plan ahead to nail down the names of everyone who will be participating on your end of the call. Blanking on someone's name in front of the group could be funny later on but it would definitely be unpleasant in the moment. After a conference call ends and the "hang up" button has been pushed, don't say anything for about five seconds. Even after the five seconds concludes, take special care to avoid saying anything you would not want someone else on the line to hear. At some point in your career you will probably be witness to a conference call hang-up malfunction, a poor choice of words that were not meant to be heard by someone on your team or the other side, and the embarrassing fall out that results from this hiccup. Following my advice on conference call hang-ups ensures there is zero chance of you ever having to deal with this fall out.

You will be working with client accounting teams during your engagements. Their accounting teams will probably consist of staff and senior accountants (generalists or specialists over specific areas), controllers and assistant controllers, VPs, and CFOs. When talking with these individuals, remember that they have their own full-time job responsibilities to worry about on top of working with you on the engagement. While the engagement is your full-time job, it will only add to their full-time workloads and stress levels. Keep this in mind as you converse with them and request support from them. You do not want to be the last straw that blows the fuse of a stressed client.

During your first six months or so on the job, ask each of your seniors or managers at the outset of each engagement if they are comfortable with you emailing the client. Some seniors will want all client communication to flow through them, while others will trust you with emailing the client directly. Do not take it personally if your senior would prefer all communication flow through him. Most seniors have had bad experiences with new associates and interns. Once he trusts that you can be relied upon he will undoubtedly give you more freedom to interact with the client, but until then let him relay all of your questions and requests to the client.

Sometimes public accounting firms have to give bad news to their clients. If your firm finds something seriously wrong, it simply must be brought up. For example, any journal entries that need to be booked related to audit findings can impact client profitability and financial statement ratios in a negative manner. Client executives are often tasked with meeting certain financial metrics during the year. Bonuses, perks, and, unfortunately, even management job security can depend on these financial metrics being met. Regardless, if an auditor finds something out of whack, he needs to bring it to the attention of management. It is obvious that management may not take auditor findings well if the findings will prevent management from receiving their bonuses, from taking their families on vacation, or even from feeling confident about their job security. These tough conversations should probably be left to the Partner or manager on the team to discuss with client management. Put yourself in the shoes of management. If an executive has already boasted to the company Board about how great the year was for the company or has already told his wife about an expensive necklace he will be able to buy her with this year's bonus, auditor findings that negatively impact the financial statements can be incredibly difficult to swallow. If you enter a tax or advisory practice, your practice group will inevitably have to deliver tough news to your clients as well. Since tough situations can bring out negative emotions in your clients, let a more experienced member of your engagement team deliver any seriously bad news to your clients.

When someone is trying to explain something to you and you are following along, nod your head or throw in some "Ah, I see" remarks to let the person speaking to you know that you understand what she is trying to convey to you. From firsthand experience I can say with confidence that your competition is exceptionally weak in this department. I see so many new associates and interns—and people in life in general, for that matter—who cannot get this basic conversational skill down. People want to feel like they are being understood when they speak. If you sit there with a blank stare on your face while your senior attempts to explain something to you, your senior's feeling of being understood is not likely to manifest. If, however, you nod along while she speaks, after the conversation concludes she will feel much better about the conversation, you, and the likelihood that the task she explained will be completed correctly.

If anyone ever tells you that she needs to "run out for an hour for an appointment" during the workday, do not press her on the nature of the appointment. If she wanted you to know, she would have told you in her original statement. You could potentially bring about an awkward situation by pressing her on it. I see so many nosy individuals press for more details when they hear these kinds of statements. A super awkward situation always follows these kinds of nosy questions. You don't want to be the person in the office who makes things awkward.

LEAPFROG PUBLIC ACCOUNTING'S LEARNING CURVE

When you hear these statements, respond with "OK, cool" and let it go at that.

Although you may be on many different engagements throughout the year, each engagement is the final exam worth 100 percent of the class grade for your clients. Your clients could have spent all year preparing for the engagement. You may view each engagement as just another day at the office, but your client definitely does not see things this way. As a way to incentivize me to take care of my teeth by brushing and flossing each night as a child, my parents made me pay for the dental repair of each cavity the dentist found at my childhood dentist appointments. As physically painful as it already was being poked and prodded by my dentist's dental instruments, I would over-analyze and stress over each word the dentist said during his review of my teeth before he told me whether or not he found any cavities at the end of the appointment. For my dentist, the appointment was just another day on the job. But for me, it was a once a year event with big ramifications. The same dynamic is true between your engagement team and the client accounting team. It is an unpleasant experience to be hounded with requests and questions by outside accountants—especially auditors. But on top of this, if your engagement team finds mistakes made by the client accounting team, client management will probably not be happy and there could be negative consequences. Your clients will probably be worried about general embarrassment, the loss of bonuses, the risk of looking incompetent, and a host of other issues. Just as dentist appointments were not fun for me, engagements are not fun for your clients. Make it a personal goal to keep this dynamic in mind and communicate with your clients accordingly during your engagements.

Never criticize your firm in public or in private. As an employee of your firm you do not have a right to criticize it. If you do not like an aspect of it, just keep it to yourself unless a Partner explicitly asks for your opinion on it. Your firm's Partners have invested their time, energy, and money into establishing and growing your firm. You would not visit another person's house and then proceed to criticize their artwork or furniture, so don't criticize another person's investment either. You should be thankful that your firm's Partners made their investments in the firm because your job has been brought into existence as a result. If something is absolutely unbearable about your firm, then that may be a good sign that you should start to explore other job options without bashing your firm in public or in private.

When communicating with coworkers who have a higher rank than you, talk in such a way that it is obvious that you acknowledge their higher rank and expertise. None of your superiors will want to be shown up by you or feel as if you are ahead of where they were when they were at your level. If you think something a senior or manager has said is incorrect, bring it up delicately and with respect if it has to be brought up at all.

If a client asks you a question that you are not exactly sure how to answer, you can always say that you need to talk to your manager before delivering a final answer back to the client. You can say that you have an idea of what the answer may be (and you can tell the client what that answer might be), but ultimately your superiors must sign off on it. Because so many accountants in industry have experience in public accounting, they are typically very understanding of new associates and interns who do not have the answers to their questions or who defer to their superiors to provide answers.

As soon as you receive a business card from someone else, write down any important or identifying features of the meeting or person on the back of the card to help your remember your new contact.

These details are usually perfect conversation starters to use in later meetings.

Never use the phrase, "As I said before." People often use this phrase as an introductory clause to repeat a matter they have previously mentioned. To my almost daily dismay I have come to the realization that most Americans cannot recognize true aggression—even when it is directed toward them—so the average American will not pick up on the belligerence behind the use of this phrase. When someone says, "As I said before" to repeat something mentioned previously, she is circuitously accusing the listener of either A) not paying attention, or B) not being bright enough to comprehend the message previously communicated. Either way, even the speaker's casual use of this phrase opens the door to potential conflict and tension between the speaker and a listener who can identify aggression. Ironically, a matter usually has to be repeated on account of the speaker's poor communicative abilities, not the listener's poor listening abilities. Since the average person out there will not pick up on the aggression behind the phrase, most people do not think twice about its use. However, you might end up working with the rare person who does think it is an aggressive phrase to use, so the courteous and polite move is to completely remove it from your vocabulary.

Rather than saying a work-paper is "complete" or "finished," say it is "ready for review." By framing the status of the work-paper this way it will not be as big of a deal to you or your senior if you have to make corrections after his review.

Public accounting is a client service industry. Client relationships ultimately keep your firm alive. Any engagement can be a tedious and annoying process for a client. Even if a client is rude or curt with you, you are never entitled to reciprocate. Maintain a respectful tone in all communications with your clients or do not say anything at all. If a client's behavior becomes unbearable, tell your Partner or manager about it. Let your Partner talk to the client about disrespectful and unprofessional behavior if he chooses to do so, but you should never fire back at the client. Burning a client relationship is probably the worst mistake anyone in public accounting could make.

When you write or correspond with a client or coworker, go out of your way to make it as easy as possible for the recipient to understand your message. For example, if you have attached multiple files to an email, it is best to give each file a label such as #1, #2, and #3. In the contents of your email, tell your recipient which information is contained within each attachment number, so it is easy for the recipient to understand your message. No one wants to receive a long email containing a dozen or more oddly named attachments with no specific reference to the attachments listed in the email message.

Never talk about client or firm information outside of its proper confines. If you have any doubt if a piece of information should be repeated, do not repeat it. Once something is out there, you cannot take it back. You will see plenty of confidential information during your public accounting career that could get you in trouble if you spread it outside of the appropriate venue. Make sure you keep it within its proper confines. Make it a general rule to say as little about your clients to outsiders as possible. Little good can come from talking about client or firm information, but a truckload of bad can result from it.

You should apply a conservative filter to how freely you allow yourself to talk at client sites. Often clients will put your engagement team in a conference room for privacy. Remember to close the conference room door when confidential information is being discussed (salary info, social security numbers, profitability numbers, etc.) so the information remains protected. When you are at a client's office, don't talk about a different client. After you leave a meeting with a client, wait until the client has left the room and the door has been shut before discussing anything that happened in the meeting. Never say anything in client elevators or waiting rooms that you would not gladly shout out on the client PA system. You never know what kind of security equipment the client has installed in its office or who may be around the corner.

Hopefully by now you know how and why to make a great first impression, the attributes of good and bad associates, how to increase your likeability at your firm, and the best and worst ways to talk to clients and coworkers. Now it is time to move on to the third section. In this section we will cover a few shortcuts, cheat codes, and general career advice to jumpstart your career in public accounting.

HOW TO TALK TO CLIENTS AND COWORKERS

SECTION 3:

CHEAT CODES & CAREER ADVICE

CHAPTER 8

THE RIGHT FIRM FIT FOR YOUR LIFE

Outside of your interpersonal skills, the right firm fit and the proper structure of your life outside of work will be the next biggest factors in your career success equation. For readers who have already signed with a firm, some of the information in this chapter may not apply to you right now, but it will if you ever decide to change firms or careers. For those of you still in school, choosing your first job may be the first time you display significant autonomy over your own life, so I hope you can use the information below to your advantage. Your firm should be a great fit for you, and your life outside of work should provide a foundation that allows success to come easy at work. If your life outside of work is chaotic and messy, it will be much harder to concentrate on producing great work at your firm. Not every firm will be the best fit for every aspiring public accountant. The firm that is the best fit for you will be so because of your particular personality and goals. Structure your life outside of work so your time at work is as enjoyable to you and as profitable to your firm as possible, and choose the job and the firm that will offer you the best life outside of work. Like yin and yang, what happens outside of the nine to five workday will impact what happens between nine and five and vice versa.

TIME COMMITMENT

Everyone in public accounting works hard. Each firm is going to ask for a significant chunk of your life every week, although some weeks may be worse than others. I have never billed more than fifty-five hours in a week, but I have had friends from other firms tell me they have billed more than ninety hours. Your hours requirements will probably be dependent upon your firm, your clients, and the types of engagements you are assigned. For example, the SEC and investors on Wall Street give publicly traded companies hard deadlines for the submission of financial reports. Because of these rigid deadlines, there can be maximum pressure on public accounting firms to issue opinions and deliverables before the deadlines. Private clients are more likely to have flexible or "softer" deadlines, but not necessarily. I find that most of the audits of smaller, private companies are mandated as part of a loan the company has received or by the private ownership of the company. It is much easier to tell a local banker or local small business owner that the audit report will be a week late than it is to give Wall Street the same message. This is one reason why associates on engagements with publicly traded clients could be forced to work many more hours than their counterparts working with private clients.

As a child I constantly heard non-accountants crack jokes about the famous accounting busy season from January 1 to April 15. Once

I entered public accounting I found that these dates can bookend a public accountant's busy season, but not necessarily so. The timing, length, and intensity of your busy seasons will be a function of your firm, your practice group, and your clients. For example, audit reports are issued throughout the year, not just between January 1 and April 15. In spite of this, many companies do have December 31 fiscal year-ends. Given the widely used December 31 year-end date, bankers and tax-preparers may want to see audited financial statements as soon after December 31 as possible each year. This is why the time period between January and April can be busy even for auditors. Try to keep busy season in mind as you evaluate job offers. For example, if you love to ski, you may want to find a firm with a busy season that is not typically in the winter months. If you love to travel to college football games in the fall, you may want to avoid firms with fall busy seasons. As you interview you should be able to gather a decent understanding of the timing of typical firm busy seasons and the intensity of the expected time commitment each week.

Keep in mind that most accounting firms pay their employees yearly salaries. You may receive bonuses and salary increases each year for a job well done during the previous year, but you probably will not be receiving overtime wages for any extra hours worked each week (unless you are an hourly intern). Some people actually enjoy working long hours. Others do not. Personally, if I had to work more than sixty hours a week for many weeks in a row, the quality of my work would begin to deteriorate and I would begin to deeply question the quality of my life. If you have held another full-time job, then you probably know how many hours per week you can work while still enjoying your life. If you are in college and have never held a full-time job, you probably do not know your hours per week limits. Try to imagine yourself working ten to fifteen hour days for many weeks in a row. Visualize how you would feel given that consistent time commitment. Ask yourself if you would totally hate your life if this was your reality, even if the money was good and the work involved enjoyable clients and engagement types. If the life you are visualizing feels like it would be miserable, a more relaxed firm with a less demanding time commitment may be a better fit for you.

FIRM CULTURE AND CLIENT EXPERIENCE

The average employee's personality will be different at every firm. During the interview process, try to get a feel for the personality of the average employee at each of your prospective firms. Each firm's company culture will probably be set from the very top - from the firm's Partners. If you can determine that a firm's Partners are more laid back through social media, references, friends who were previous employees, or other means, then you can bet that vibe will trickle down and run throughout the rest of the firm. If the Partners are more serious and demanding, then the rest of the firm probably will be as well. If I were interviewing, I would try to get the feel for a firm's culture by talking to a former employee of the prospective firm or by reading company reviews online. Some people enjoy a rigid work environment with lots of structure. Others prefer a more free-flowing atmosphere. Some people like to work with serious coworkers, while others would rather work with a more playful and laid-back group. No firm personality is inherently wrong, but you should aim for the firm atmosphere that most closely aligns with your personality.

Many start-ups and smaller companies will only have space in their budgets for one accounting or finance employee. This person will wear all the hats of the accounting and finance department. This utility player may be involved in fund-raising efforts (as a normal CFO would be) while also performing the bank reconciliation each month (as a normal staff accountant would). I really enjoyed working with these kinds of clients as an auditor. I learned the most by working with them because they wear so many hats. However, these utility players will most likely only exist at small companies. In theory the larger a company becomes, the more personnel it will need in its accounting department. Also, if you work on an engagement with a large company as an intern or associate, you might not have as much interaction with the upper level client management team due to the probable size and depth of the large company's accounting team. If you work on a smaller client, you might have a great shot at working with the client's CFO or controller. You may not be able to get a straight answer when you are interviewing, but you might want to ask each prospective firm about the client personnel that you will typically be working with while on an average engagement.

Your work experience will be heavily dictated by your firm's clients. For example, if the support provided by the client is all that is actually needed, on the audit of a small private client an associate can complete her testing of multiple client balance sheet accounts in one day. I have seen audit associates start and complete their testing of a small private client's cash, receivables, and prepaid expenses in less than nine hours. Signing off on this many accounts in a single day probably wouldn't occur on the audit of a large publicly traded company. On the audits of large companies, associates can spend many weeks auditing just one trial balance account. As a general rule I like to think that while working on large clients, associates will probably spend more time on the specific accounts they have been assigned to audit, but they will probably not see as wide of an account spectrum as associates and interns assigned to small clients. I have only worked in audit, but this depth versus breadth phenomenon could be consistent on many tax and advisory jobs as well. The trade-off will vary at every firm and by engagement, so I recommend that you ask about the depth and breadth of the experience you might expect to receive as an employee as you interview at each of your prospective firms.

COMPENSATION AND BENEFITS

In addition to base salary, there are a few other factors to consider when weighing the financial aspects of job offers. The cost of living in different cities across the United States can vary dramatically. For example, one dollar in New York City is worth much less than one dollar in Jackson, Mississippi. A $50,000 salary in Jackson probably gets a single person just as far a $150,000 salary in Manhattan. If you have job offers in multiple cities, think about the cost of living within each city to better compare the salaries of the job offers. If you are confused about the cost of living in a potential city, go to a real estate website and check out the asking prices of average looking homes in the city. When it comes to salaries, don't just think about the size of the base salary. Ask yourself what you could do with that number and the quality of life the number would give you in each prospective location.

Outside of your mortgage/rent and any student loan payments, your health insurance could be your largest monthly expenditure once you enter the work force. I am 26 years old and in the best shape of my life. I have not visited a doctor on account of an illness in over four years and have taken less than half a sick day in the last two years. Yet somehow my health insurance costs me around $550 each month—after tax! The cost of health care in the U.S. is outrageous, but many people in their twenties do not realize how much health insurance will cost them once they leave their parents' plans. I say all this to emphasize that you should definitely ask about health insurance before signing an offer letter from any prospective firm. Some firms offer health insurance without taking a dime out of your paycheck. This will save you thousands of dollars each year. Other firms will take something out of your paycheck for health insurance or maybe not offer health insurance at all. This benefit is too big of a factor to dismiss when you are evaluating job offers.

Residents of some states pay sizable state income taxes. Other states do not have state income taxes. If you are evaluating job offers between firms in different states, this is definitely something you will need to evaluate.

Tax advantaged retirement plans and employer matching provisions are two financial tools which most young people unfortunately often don't consider when they are evaluating job offers. Think about employer matching provisions as free income to you. One of the most costly financial mistakes one can make is to fail to contribute to a tax advantaged retirement plan that includes an employer matching feature. Anything you can stash away in your twenties in a tax advantaged retirement account will hopefully be worth many times more in your retirement. Forty years from now you will be happy you took the time to think about stashing something away for the future.

There are also several types of bonuses to keep in mind. Signing, spot, referral, and annual are four of the major types you may see in public accounting. Signing bonuses represent amounts paid to you for signing your offer letter and committing to the firm. Usually you will receive a portion of the total signing bonus upon signing and another portion after the completion of a certain amount of time at the firm. Spot bonuses are sporadic bonuses usually paid for doing a great job over a stretch of time or on a particular engagement. Spot bonuses are fairly rare in public accounting. Referral bonuses are paid for recruiting someone to join your firm or for landing a client. It is incredibly expensive to find and onboard new hires, so many employers offer handsome referral bonuses to incentivize employees to assist in recruiting efforts. Referral bonuses can be as high as the newly recruited employee's first month's salary. Annual bonuses are typically paid at the end of the firm's fiscal year and are usually a reward for a job well done during the previous year. The total of these bonuses over the course of a year can be sky-high, so keep potential bonuses in mind when evaluating the compensation of different job offers.

Last, and least (in terms of compensation), don't forget about potential cell phone or other fringe reimbursements. Some firms will help you with your monthly cell phone bill if you use your phone for work. This reimbursement can result in hundreds, if not thousands, of dollars saved each year while employed.

TRAVEL, TRAINING, AND BRAND RECOGNITION

The ability to travel and work abroad while employed will also be determined by your firm's client roster. If your firm has clients all over the world, the chance you could travel internationally for work is fairly high. If your firm only has small clients in your town, you probably will not be traveling very often. Some people love to travel and cherish the experience, while others would rather stay put. This is another topic to ask about while interviewing. It will vary by firm, practice group, and engagement.

One of the possible advantages of signing with an international firm is the world-wide brand recognition it might have. Most people in the accounting and finance world have heard of the big accounting firms. If you join a local firm and interview elsewhere after your time at the local firm comes to a close, there is a high likelihood that your interviewer will not be familiar with your previous firm. As your career progresses this could present some challenges that associates and interns from larger firms do not have to worry about.

Larger firms typically provide standard training sessions for new hires at the outset of their careers. My brother spent a week in Orlando for a training session at the beginning of his career with an international accounting firm. These formal trainings can be a great way to become acclimated to your firm's expectations. Most small firms do not have the scale to support this allocation of resources, so most new hire training will be completed on the job. Formal training can be a big deal to some people and not matter at all to others. This is another area that you should weigh in proportion to the effect you think it will have on you.

TIME OFF

Almost all accounting firms offer at least two weeks of paid vacation per year, and some firms will even offer up to five weeks of vacation. Remember that a week is only five days in this situation, not seven. Calculate your annual salary on a weekly basis and use that number to determine how valuable these weeks off can be.

Sick days are another benefit you should inquire about when interviewing. Some firms offer unlimited or weeks of paid sick time. Other firms might make you use your vacation time after only a few sick days. Given recent advances in technology, it is almost as easy for most public accountants to work from home as it is from the office. All you will need to complete much of your work is a computer and an internet connection. Even when you are out sick your firm might ask you to complete a certain amount of work from home. If you are prone to illness, you will want to think seriously about firm sick time policies when weighing prospective firms against each other.

If you think you might be adding a baby to your family in the near future, *delicately* try to find out about your prospective firms' paternity or maternity leave policies. By *delicately*, I mean that you should keep in mind that some employers (outside of any legal implications) may be incentivized to hire a person who will not need to take months of paid time off over someone who might need to take a significant amount of paid time off for maternity or paternity leave. Of all the firm time off and benefits policies, I've found that maternity and paternity leave vary the most from company to company. Some companies might offer months of paid time off, while others might offer only a few weeks or no paid time off at all. You rarely will see this wide of a spectrum in other types of time off policies.

Your ability to enjoy your life outside of work will be handicapped if you are spending your days working at a place you dislike. However, if you're already employed, I would advise you to give your current employer at least a year of your life—even if you are not in love with the place. Your firm took a risk by hiring you, and the loyalty you show by sticking around is laudable. In addition, your opinion of your life at your firm might totally change as you settle into your firm. At the end of my first day as an associate I actually had some semi-serious thoughts about quitting the next day. Nevertheless, I decided to stick it out and could not have been happier with my decision.

THE RIGHT FIRM FIT FOR YOUR LIFE

Now that you are thinking about the characteristics of the firm that is the best fit for you, we will turn our focus to giving you the best chance to not just identify but actually sign with the firm which will offer you the best chance of experiencing success in your accounting career.

CHAPTER 9

RÉSUMÉS AND INTERVIEWING

You give yourself the best chance of finding the firm that is the right fit for you by having a stellar résumé and the ability to thrive in interviews. Without a great résumé and interview skills, you are unlikely to receive many job offers. I have reviewed hundreds of résumés and interviewed with dozens of firms. Below are my best tips to give you the greatest chance to land a job at the firm that is best for you.

RÉSUMÉ TIPS

Whether you are applying for your first job in accounting or applying for a new job after a few years of experience, your résumé will be a crucial part of your job search process. Sometimes firms receive hundreds of résumés for one opening. It is best to assume that to whittle down the pool, any résumé with an error will be immediately thrown out of the stack. You have to ensure your résumé is clean, crisp, and free of any errors or typos. A prospective firm will develop its first impression of you based on your résumé, and first impressions are everything in the job search process. Send your résumé to three friends to review for grammatical errors and typos before you submit it to any prospective employers. If you are a recent college grad, not listing your college GPA will be a red flag in your prospective firm's eyes. If you have been working for a few years, you probably do not need to list your college GPA unless it was a 3.50 or higher. Never exceed one page with your résumé. Keep it clean, organized, and straight-forward. Use a professional font and black ink only. Some experts say to write a blurb about the job you are seeking at the top of your résumé. I do not think this is necessary. I think the extra blurb does more harm than good by creating more room for grammatical errors and mishaps.

BEFORE THE INTERVIEW

The number one piece of advice I give is that you have to know exactly what you want when interviewing. Someone with a 3.0 GPA who knows exactly what he wants is probably more likely to get the job than another person with a 4.0 who is not sure about what he wants. After your interview is over, your interviewer should know exactly what you want, why you want it, and why the job is the perfect vehicle to take you where you want to go. Research the company and the job opening before you apply. Find unique and specific characteristics about the job and company that you will be able to leverage to achieve your professional and personal goals. Work these unique characteristics into why the job and company are the perfect match to help you get to where you want to go. If you cannot do this or find it hard to do so, maybe the potential position is not the right one for you. My firm once put an associate candidate through multiple rounds of interviews and an interview lunch. After he departed that afternoon, everyone who had interviewed him met for a candidate debrief. All of us had positive things to say about the candidate, but the number one quality that continued to be brought up was that he knew exactly what he wanted. It aligned perfectly with the job he was seeking. The perfect marriage of what he wanted and the open position made for too good of a story. He was offered the job and started two weeks later.

Think of your upcoming interview as a two way street: you are getting to know the firm and the firm is getting to know you. There is no need to stress out. View each interview as simply a chance to make a new connection and expand your network, rather than a test on how you measure up as a prospective employee or a judgment of your worth as a person. If you are pursuing an associate or intern position, you should definitely know the basics of accounting. On the other hand, do not freak yourself out worrying about not having the answers to technical questions that might come up in your interview. Whenever I meet a prospective hire, my goal is to find out if I would enjoy working with the person in a dumpster fire engagement. I look for fit and interpersonal skills over technical skills. Technical questions may not even be brought up in many of your interviews, so do not stress out about them. If an interviewee knows the basics, technical skills can always be taught later on. And remember, not receiving a job offer can be a bigger blessing than receiving one.

As a way to get your mind right before each interview, visualize each interview as a golden opportunity with unlimited upside and zero downside. Even if the worst-case scenario occurs and you are not offered the job, you gain valuable experience just by venturing into a new office and meeting new people. You will be that much sharper for your next interview. Due to circumstances and factors outside of your control, the odds of success are always going to be slim. I've seen dozens of quality candidates turned down who probably would have been offered jobs if the timing of their applications had only been a few weeks earlier or later. Firm hiring needs can come and go at a moment's notice due to any number of factors that are outside of your control. There are a million and one reasons why you will not get the job offer (or sale, nomination, etc.) which have nothing to do with you or your preparation, so don't let a negative result bring you down and throw you off track in your pursuit of the next opportunity which comes your way.

DURING THE INTERVIEW

You have to tell a great story in your interview. As discussed earlier, human brains are hard-wired to connect to stories. Your interviewer should come away with a story of how you got to where you are currently, why you want this specific job at this specific firm, and what you want to do with the job and firm once you are hired. You need to make it easy for your interviewer to sell you and your story during her post interview discussions with the rest of the firm. Remember that by vouching for you, your interviewer is sticking her neck out for you. If you turn out to be a bad hire, you will be a poor reflection on her. No interviewer wants to stick her neck out for someone who could be a tough sell or who could embarrass her after joining the firm, so try to interview accordingly.

Usually your interviewer will begin with a few pleasantries followed by several questions. Your answers to your interviewer's questions should give both of you plenty of foundation upon which to build the rest of your conversation. Never respond with "yes" or "no." After each of her questions have been answered, your interviewer will want you to ask her questions. Do not think that by asking questions you are selfishly taking up her time. You will look unprepared and uninterested in the firm if you do not bring your own questions to the interview table. If you cannot keep asking questions until time runs out, make sure you ask three questions at a minimum. I have listed a few questions below that you can ask any firm and practice group. The answers to these questions should give you a better idea of what your day-to-day life might be like if employed by the firm. As you prepare for each interview you can come up with other questions that are perfectly tailored to your prospective firms.

Questions for any firm or practice group

1. What industries are your firm's clients typically found within?
2. What unique attributes of these industries do you enjoy?
3. Who and how large are your typical clients (if you can talk about it)?
4. How many people are on the average engagement team on a typical client?
5. Given your firm's typical client base, what time of year is your firm's usual "Busy Season" if one exists?
6. What types of client personnel do you end up working with on most of your engagements?
7. How are engagements and engagement teams scheduled?
8. What is your favorite aspect of the firm? (Do not waste your time asking about the interviewer's least favorite aspect of the firm - you will not get the real answer)

LEAPFROG PUBLIC ACCOUNTING'S LEARNING CURVE

9   Where have the last few employees who have left the firm gone?

Other Tips

1   Do not bring up compensation during the interview. You can ask about benefits, but I would avoid any salary discussions. Save any salary discussions until after the firm makes you an offer.
2   Do not talk about drugs, alcohol, sex, ex's, hangovers, or politics.
3   Do not say anything negative about any person, company, food, or current event. You never know who is best friends with your interviewer or whose dad owns which company.
4   Keep asking questions until time runs out.

If an interviewer ever asks about your biggest weakness, you may want to start focusing on another firm. We all know that nobody gives a straight answer to these "biggest weakness" questions, and any firm who asks questions like these is apparently not serious about living in reality. You do not have time to waste in life by interacting with people who do not strive for an accurate perception of reality. The "biggest weakness" questions send both the interviewer and the interviewee straight into a fantasyland. I am beginning to believe that some companies ask job candidates about their biggest weaknesses in order to evaluate how proficient they are at lying, since lying may be an integral part of the jobs they are seeking. Anybody who has been in the working world for more than a few months knows the biggest weakness which is stated in response to these "weakness" oriented questions will *not* be the biggest weakness exposed during the first few weeks of any new hire's career.

Prospective firms might take you out to eat during the interview process. Even though the firm will cover the bill, never order any of the most expensive items on the menu. The firm will definitely pay attention to your order, as it will be a test of your personal judgment. Obviously you also want to display decent table manners while out to eat. I have found that most people interested in public accounting have decent table manners, but I will occasionally see two major mistakes when I dine with prospective hires:

1. Eating before everyone else at the table has been served.
2. Holding silverware incorrectly. If you do not know how to properly hold a spoon, fork, or knife, there are plenty of videos on the internet that can show you how it is properly done.

AFTER THE INTERVIEW

At the conclusion of each interview, ask for your interviewer's business card or contact information. Even if you are certain you would never want to work at the prospective company, make a point to write a thank you note or email to your interviewers after each interview. This is another action that has huge upside and zero downside. You will stand out among the other candidates without question if you do, and your thank you note may be the ultimate tiebreaker that gives you the job offer over a competitor.

You may want to reach out to clients or former employees of potential firms to get their opinions, especially if you have great connections. This can be the perfect way to obtain third-party information through the eyes of someone with real life experience working with or for the firms on your list. As you talk to those with experience dealing with or working for your prospective firms, keep in mind that a national firm's office in one city may be totally different than its office located in another city.

Read the online reviews of each of your prospective firms. Be cautioned, though—similar to other online reviews of restaurants, hotels, apartments, etc., often only a certain personality type or a former employee who has had a poor experience will take the time to leave an online review. I can honestly say the few negative online reviews of my former employers have been total garbage. I think many internet reviews are written by disgruntled former employees who have left on poor terms.

If you follow the advice above, you will hopefully be able to get a great job at a great firm. However, finding the right gig is just the starting point of your career. Once you start working at your job, then the rat race will officially begin. The remaining chapters of this section exist to help you make the most of your time once you begin your career.

CHAPTER 10

WORKPLACE BEST PRACTICES

In this chapter I want to discuss a few general workplace best practices. Most of this is anecdotal advice that I found worked for me during my time as an intern and associate. Some of it will need to be tailored to your specific job and workplace environment, but your career learning curve should be shortened significantly if you act on the suggestions below.

DURING YOUR FIRST DAYS IN THE RAT RACE

Beware of relying on the advice or "wisdom" of other interns and associates. Your firm's intern and associate class probably will contain the typical loud mouth who is a smooth talker but a poor performer. Often those who talk the loudest possess the least competence. You do not want to be steered down the wrong road on a task by an intern or associate only to be told that you are going the wrong way by a senior or manager. You never want to throw anyone else under the bus (even when it's justified), so you would just have to eat the mistake. You can minimize the risk of this happening by listening to seniors and managers more than fellow interns and associates.

In order to quickly learn the names of your coworkers (especially the Partner and manager groups), take advantage of your firm's web page. Your firm's website might display headshots of your firm's management team and list the related first and last names. Print out the headshots and related names and pin them up in your house in a place where you will frequently see them. This is a fantastic way for your subconscious to begin absorbing faces and names. If the names of management are not easy to print, print the headshots of your management team and write their names on the page before pinning the document on your wall. Some firms will produce an annual firm directory containing pictures and names of firm employees. If your firm produces a directory you should ask for it and use it to your advantage.

Most firms will produce a document that spells out firm expectations by employee level. It may include expectations in regards to character traits, technical expertise, hours worked, and business development. If your firm produces one of these documents, print it out and pin it up at your house in a location where you will see it regularly. During your first couple of months at work just focus on meeting firm expectations at the associate/intern level. Once you feel like you have the job requirements and expectations down related to your current level, try to begin meeting the expectations of the next level. Aim to become one percent better at your job each day. These one percent increments will eventually begin to compound, and after a short period you will be significantly more advanced than where you began on your first day.

Organize all of your firm-issued training materials, IT walk-through guides, and any other standard "self-help" files in a folder on your desktop that you can quickly and easily locate. These materials are usually tailor-made for new associates and interns. You don't want to become the annoying new hire who consistently asks the same questions over and over again about standard job activities and procedures that are already detailed in these materials.

Your firm will probably provide you with a laptop and one extra portable monitor. This is great, but you will probably find that you are exponentially more productive when working with three or more monitors instead of two. Your office may be filled with workstations that have stationary monitors. With your laptop, your spare portable monitor, and the stationary monitor at each of your office workstations, you can have the luxury of three screens at your office. However, at client sites you will only have two monitors (if you only bring your laptop and your firm-issued portable screen to client sites). When I first began my career I worked at a painfully slower rate at client sites than at the office because I only had two screens at client sites instead of three. After many inefficient days spent at clients, it dawned on me that I actually had a giant monitor from college in the back of my closet at home. I decided to take my personal monitor with me to the client site the next day in addition to my firm-issued portable monitor. The next day at the client site was exceptionally productive, and the rest was audit history. My personal monitor is actually so large that it will not fit in a backpack or briefcase, so I had to carry it by hand to client sites. No one at my firm had ever seen an associate bring a giant personal monitor to a client site in order to have three screens. I would like to think that bringing the third monitor contributed to building the perception that I was someone who cared about working efficiently and effectively. Many of my clients had seen auditors with two screens before, but they were not prepared for the sight of the giant third monitor. In addition to making me hyper productive, the giant monitor was a fantastic conversation-starter with clients. You may want to buy a spare personal monitor if you find that you are more productive when using more than two computer screens. My personal monitor cost only $20, and your firm may reimburse you for money spent on a third monitor. Nevertheless, I would advise against buying a third monitor until you see the equipment your firm provides, and remember to check the plug-in options on your firm-issued computer so you don't buy a monitor that is incompatible.

Once you receive your firm-issued laptop, select a conservative desktop wallpaper. Your coworkers and clients will not be able to help but notice your desktop background after spending hours working with you, so choose a picture with their possible perceptions of it in mind. Wallpapers related to alcohol, drugs, sex, tobacco, TV shows, movies, or cartoons are not the best choices. Even if these are clean images, they could be perceived as goofy by your coworkers and clients. A picture of a scenic landscape or a family photograph is always acceptable.

WHEN AT CLIENT SITES

Clients might give you access to their company snack bar and coffee machine. I enjoy snacking while working and probably have taken advantage of more client snack bars than any other accountant in America. Snack bars and coffee machines are great, but do not utilize them unless your client has given you permission to do so.

If someone you are unacquainted with ever walks into the room where you are working, stop what you are doing, stand up, and introduce yourself to her. You want to show as much courtesy and respect as possible to clients without breaching independence. Standing up to introduce yourself will elevate you in the eyes of your clients and your engagement team. Depending on the formality of the circumstances, you may want to stand up anytime a client walks in the room even if you are already acquainted. When working at client sites I stand up each morning when the client contact first enters the room. If the contact is constantly bouncing in and out of the room, it would be unnecessary and awkward for you to keep standing each time she enters the room. You will have to gauge how often you stand based on the circumstances, but you can't go wrong by standing when unfamiliar clients first enter the room or when the familiar client contacts first enter your team room each morning. The same rule applies during your first few weeks at work with your new coworkers. If someone ever takes the time to walk over to your desk and introduce herself, stand up to talk to her. Not everyone stands up anymore, but anytime I introduce myself to new hires I notice immediately how big of a difference standing up makes. If the new hire remains seated, the conversation feels awkward and painful. If he stands up, then my first perception of him totally transforms. Standing up to greet millennials may not be that big of a deal, but to baby boomers (your Partners and client executives) standing up could be a very big deal.

Do not work on or talk about another client's engagement in front of a different client. Any client will want to see you working on his engagement in order to feel better about the hefty fees he pays your firm for your accounting services. Even if zero support has been provided, he may begin to question your firm's fees if he thinks your attention is not purely focused on his engagement.

Try your best to avoid being late to a client meeting. You would rather be late to a meeting with another member of your firm than with a client.

Clients come before everything else. Keeping an organized calendar will help you stay on top of all your commitments and minimize the chance of mistakenly missing a meeting.

Some days you may have to spend a lot of time just waiting on the client to send you support. Try to use this free time to your advantage. Do not waste it away surfing the web or scrolling through your social media. Enter your hours, study for the CPA exams, finish up any loose ends from earlier jobs, or try to get ahead on another project. Anything you can knock off your to-do list during the slow period will be one less item to worry about when things get busy.

Lastly, remember the pressure is ultimately on your client to provide your firm with the support needed to complete the engagement. Your client may terminate the relationship with your firm if things go poorly, but if the client terminates the relationship before the engagement is complete then he will not receive the opinion or deliverable he badly needs. Obviously you will have to do some digging, but at the end of the day it is up to your client to show your firm what it needs to see in order to finalize the engagement. Many public accountants become weighed down with anxiety over matters that are actually their clients' problems. After you have done all you can do to push your engagement to completion, try not to waste your energy worrying about an issue that is actually your client's problem.

BEST BUSINESS IQ AND DEVELOPMENT PRACTICES

Stay current on financial/accounting trends by reading books, magazines, and websites in your off time. It will not be a good look for you if you are exposed as being completely unaware of a major event or trend in the economy. Following the social media accounts of the major financial news providers will help you stay current on major events without applying much effort on your part.

Subscribe to your town's local business journal, especially if you're not originally from the area. Many business journals in big cities now send daily email blasts that cover the most important events of the previous day. You want to be plugged into the commercial activity in your area, and this is a very easy way to become informed. Each morning you can open your email, quickly read over the previous day's major business events, and move on with your day. When these events are later brought up around your office or at client sites, you will have a better understanding of the conversations and your clients and coworkers will be impressed by how in tune you are with the business activity in your city.

During your associate years be thinking about developing accounting specialties in niche areas that will set you up for success in the future. Try to align the work you enjoy with what you think will be in demand in the coming years. The more you specialize in a needed area the more indispensable you become. You will have a better ability to win new clients as a manager and you will make your path to Partner much easier. Or, maybe another company or client will notice your expertise and want to hire you. Either way, you open yourself up to more windfalls and opportunities through specialization. Whether that specialization is in a specific service-line, a certain industry, or a technical expertise, you will become more valuable to your firm and to the outside marketplace by specializing. As a new associate I repeatedly noticed that many of the managers at my firm would seek the counsel of one particular senior associate regarding technical questions which popped up in their employee benefit plan (EBP) audits. I soon discovered that this senior was widely known as the EBP guru within my firm. He was probably second only to a few of our firm's Partners and managers in terms of EBP expertise. He led our firm's weekly EBP audit meetings and was generally seen as the go-to guy for questions related to EBP audits. Somehow he had developed an insanely high level of expertise over EBP audits in just a few years of public accounting experience. I still am not quite sure how he gained this level of expertise in this one area so quickly, but his specialized skill obviously was an asset to the firm and to him professionally. By specializing you make your firm more valuable, increase your job security, and gain the ability to leverage your expertise if you ever decide to make a career change. You may not be able to be an EBP audit guru, but look for other areas in which you can develop a niche expertise to benefit both your firm and yourself. Maybe your firm focuses on one industry, one service-line, or has one particularly large client that you could claim a specialty within. Specializing definitely will not be easy, but there is no doubt that it will pay huge dividends at every stage of your career.

Learn to play golf. Whether you like it or not, many business deals are done on the golf course and the sport presents an amazing opportunity to bond with your coworkers and business contacts. Your coworkers may simply enjoy playing for recreation, or members of your firm may be asked to play with existing or prospective clients. You do not want to sell yourself short by not having the ability to play. Do not think that you have to be a professional to play either. Sign up for a couple of lessons from a pro if you have never played before. You will be shocked by how much more you can improve through a one-hour lesson from a pro than from a full weekend at the practice range by yourself. You don't have to be a great golfer to be able to hang with your coworkers or clients—just try to get the ball in the air and don't take yourself or your game too seriously. Everyone hits poor shots every once in a while. Whatever you do, don't get upset or throw a fit on the course after a bad shot. This would be a terrible look, and it would be better for you to not play at all.

Whenever a coworker terminates employment with your firm, make sure you get his contact information before he leaves your firm and you lose touch. You may need to contact him in the future if you are searching for a new job, trying to make a sale, or if you are just visiting his new town and want to meet up for a drink or a bite to eat. You want to have as large of a personal contact database as possible. Having someone's contact info can't hurt you, but it could be incredibly beneficial to have in the future. Many of your coworkers will send an office-wide email on their last day with their personal contact information. You should do the same if you ever leave your firm.

PHYSICAL CONSIDERATIONS

Buy a pair of computer glasses. Before I discovered computer glasses my eyes would dry out, turn red, and I would see spots at the end of the day from the hours spent staring at my computer screen. Thanks to computer glasses my eyes feel amazing even after a long day of working on my computer. You could also develop a reputation as a trendsetter in your office by being the first person to wear them. Protecting your eyes will increase your ability to concentrate and work longer hours. Remember to make a point to look away from the computer screen every twenty minutes or so and blink a few times before looking at your screen again. This will reduce eye strain commonly associated with working on a computer.

LEAPFROG PUBLIC ACCOUNTING'S LEARNING CURVE

You need a great night's sleep each night to make the most out of each day at work. If you are not sleeping well, you may find that you sleep better by copying my standard bedtime routine. I try to avoid any computer or cell phone screens for at least a half hour before going to sleep. I sleep best in a totally dark, pitch-black room, so I unplug all electronics and turn off all lights in and around my room each night. I place my cell phone in a different room to distance myself from any radiation or electromagnetic frequencies. I only developed this routine a couple of years ago. My sleep has become more pure, and I wake up way more mentally clear and alive.

If you must use tobacco, limit any smoking or chewing tobacco use to as little as possible. There is almost no upside, if any, for people to see or smell tobacco on you at work, but there can be a massive downside. If you have to smoke in the mornings, do it in a separate set of clothes or before your morning shower. You will not make any friends at your office or at the client site by coming in with the stench of cigarette smoke surrounding you. If you have been using tobacco for years, your sense of smell may be dulled. Don't make your coworkers' workdays unbearable on account of your use of the devil's dirt. And yes, some people feel like they must use tobacco to reduce work-related stress—I get it. If this is the case, just aim to curtail your use to the most discreet level you can handle. Limiting your use to only well before and after work would be a good place to start. You and your coworkers will be thankful.

Carry extra personal hygiene products and office supplies in your backpack, briefcase, or car so you are prepared when the unexpected happens to you or one of your coworkers. Extra pens and pencils, eyedrops, an umbrella, immune system boosters, extra batteries, hand sanitizer, and a phone charger can all be total game changers. You will come across as a dependable and responsible employee if you can offer your coworkers one of these items when they are in dire need of it.

Always brush your teeth and use mouthwash before work. If you know you occasionally suffer from bad breath, leave an extra bottle of mouthwash in your car for any emergency situations. You will frequently be sitting near your team members and clients while huddled around the same laptop or computer. It is torture to deal with someone's bad breath while you both are circled around a single computer.

Almost all of your coworkers will listen to music through headphones while working. I didn't expect this when I entered the workforce as an intern. Since everyone else listened to music while working, I thought I might give it a try. I quickly discovered that I could not listen to music with vocals while working on projects that required lots of typing. If I listened to songs with lyrics while working, I would often find myself typing the words of the songs instead of the words I needed to type. You may experience the same phenomenon when working. I enjoyed studying to Miles Davis and John Coltrane in college and have found that listening to them while working on complex tasks was beneficial. If I am ever attempting to complete a repetitive task or something that required less mental effort, I go with something more high energy and can handle vocals.

DAY TO DAY OFFICE WISDOM

If you have to ask a general question at work, try to ask a coworker who actually enjoys coaching others and avoid asking someone who prefers to solely focus on his own projects. Some people actually enjoy helping the less experienced with general questions and problems related to the job, while others make it obvious that they are not in love with coaching the less experienced. One of my former coworkers had previously been a football coach at the Texas high school football powerhouse Westlake High School. In line with his coaching background, from my first time working with him it was obvious that he actually enjoyed teaching others and providing answers to the various questions interns and associates inevitably run into while getting their feet wet. Everyone at the firm (especially the Partners) noticed his attitude, and he was probably the most well-liked employee at our firm. This is the way to be when you become experienced enough to answer questions, even if you are an introvert or simply prefer to focus only on your own assignments. Some of your coworkers will make it obvious that they prefer to solely focus on their own assignments. This is fine, but as a new hire you should take note of this attitude and direct your questions to a coworker who will enjoy showing you the ropes.

If you have been at a particular task for more than twenty minutes and believe that you have not made much progress, it may be best to stop what you are doing, circle the wagons with your senior or manager on the engagement, and together analyze the best way for you to proceed. Some assignments, even when attempted by the most seasoned Partners, will be completed at a glacial pace, but others in theory should be completed quickly. The following is a sentence I like to use when I have hit a roadblock on an assignment and need direction from a superior: "Hey senior, I've spent the last twenty minutes or so totally spinning my wheels on this project. Any chance I could come to your desk and run a few things by you whenever you have a moment?" If you know the conversation will last more than a few minutes, make sure your senior knows that you are not anticipating a quick fifteen-second conversation. You can say, "Hey, this might take a few minutes. Is now a good time to talk, or would another time be better?" You don't want your senior thinking that she has to spoon-feed you, but no one wants you to burn a hole in the budget by getting hung up on a task for too long either. The time versus progress balancing act will be something that you have get the feel for on each job and with each engagement team.

At the beginning of my career I had several unfortunate experiences in which I spent a significant amount of time testing support that ultimately did not tie to the trial balance. This was a total waste of time. In each instance after I realized the support did not tie out, I had to request new support (which tied to the trial balance) and start over. Unfortunately auditors simply cannot do much with bad support. For readers going into audit: do not work with support until you are reasonably certain that it ties to the trial balance. If you can, tie all support out to the trial balance before performing any other work. For those going into tax and advisory: the point I want to emphasize is to avoid working with support unless you are reasonably certain that it is the support your firm needs to obtain.

When you're writing an email, only enter the recipient's email address into the "Send To" box when your typed message is complete and ready to be sent. This will prevent you from accidentally sending a halfway written email. If no recipient is entered in the "Send To" box, it is impossible for your email to be sent. I cannot tell you how many times this tactic has saved me from accidentally sending an embarrassing, halfway written email to a client or coworker.

Each time you come across a word or phrase which is unfamiliar to you, stop, look it up, and write it down. This practice will be a minor irritant in the short run but you will reap dividends from it in the long run. Your firm will probably use a certain set of tick-marks in firm work-papers and documentation. Tick-marks confused me at the beginning of my career, but after a few weeks of interaction they seemed wildly elementary. Tick-marks exist to quickly communicate a step performed or a piece of information necessary to understand documentation. As a new hire, take the time to create a personal databank of all of your firm's tick-marks and their respective meanings. This may take a few minutes, but it will greatly cut down on the confusion that comes with seeing an unfamiliar tick-mark. Any time you see a tick-mark you do not recognize, add it and its definition to your databank once you understand its meaning. When you see the same tick-mark later on and cannot quite remember the meaning, it will be much easier to pop open your tick-mark databank than to search for the work-paper in which you last saw the tick-mark.

As an associate or intern you will frequently find yourself working on multiple projects at a time. You will start an original project, make progress, and then kick questions or support requests back to the client. While waiting for the client to respond, you will probably start working on another task for a different area of the engagement or perhaps for an entirely different client. Superstar associates and interns create and maintain open item lists for all of their projects and clients. After taking a task or a project as far as they can for the time being, a great associate will make a list of the questions and support needed to push the task or project to completion. After you find yourself knee-deep in multiple projects for the first time, you will realize how easy it is to forget or mix-up the status of the multiple projects you have touched. Open item lists prove to be invaluable when, after spending several days working on other projects, your manager asks you about the status of an earlier task. If you keep open item lists, you can simply pop open your list to go through it with her or email it to her directly. You want to avoid frittering away precious time by digging through your original project in an attempt to piece together the project's status while your manager waits for an answer. Also, you should write the date you last asked the client for support on every open item list you compile. This will help your manager and you determine the appropriate time to follow-up so you do not come off as too aggressive or lackadaisical.

Take care to organize and label support to make it as easy as possible for your reviewer to review your work. If you worked with a massive amount of support, you may want to walk through how you organized it with your senior to save him time on the backend (if you will be unavailable during his review). It is very frustrating for seniors to review your work if they can't find your support. Labeling support files with dates, contract numbers, invoice numbers, or names can be very helpful. Your senior does not want to waste time opening up file after file of unlabeled support in an effort to find the one file needed to review your work. Consider creating a support folder for each work-paper or a different folder for each type of support. If you take the few moments to do this for each task (especially without being told) you will skyrocket to all-star staff status in the eyes of your engagement team.

Begin every morning by attacking the most complex or arduous assignment on your to-do list for the day. Save the easier, less mentally taxing items for the late afternoon and evening. The same goes for having difficult conversations with clients and coworkers. Hit the most painful task on your to-do list first while your mind is fresh and get it out of the way. If you have worked hard during the day, then your mental facilities will slow by the end of the day. This is the ideal time to be taking on the less challenging tasks and the work which you are more comfortable tackling, not the biggest challenges of the day.

Make it a habit to write down how you spent your time at the end of each day. At most firms employee timesheets are due every Monday for the previous week. Don't get caught on Monday trying to remember the amount of time you spent working on different tasks during the previous week. You will not be able to remember and the time you record will be inaccurate. You can avoid all of this by making a habit of writing down how you spent your time at the end of each workday.

LONG TERM CONSIDERATIONS

Use all the vacation days your firm gives you each year. Vacation days are good for you and exist for a reason. You won't gain any brownie points with your firm by not using them. Your firm would like for you to take these days off to unwind, relax, and put your work-life metric back into balance. Your mind needs these vacation days to decompress and rest. Book them as far in advance as possible and remind your team as your vacation approaches so no one is thrown off when you are out of the office. Also, when one of your coworkers is on vacation, try to leave him alone unless the situation is an emergency. No one wants to be bothered with trivial work related matters while on vacation time.

Do not pursue any office romance. Romantic relationships can be against company policy at many firms, and a bad argument or break up could have serious professional and legal consequences. Office romance simply adds a new level of complexity to the job that would ideally not exist. I have only seen one office romance in my career which I thought was a great situation, and that couple consisted of the two most mature and solid millennials in America. If you really believe deep down that you have found "the one" at your firm and your firm is not on board with your relationship, it would not be too hard for one of you to find a new job given your accounting backgrounds.

If you are headed into public accounting directly after college graduation (especially if you are single), you may begin seeing symptoms of the illness that I like to call "Fluffy's Disease." As a new associate or intern you will begin receiving handsome paychecks every two weeks, maybe for the first time in your life. You might be tempted to adopt a fun and "fluffy" pet—cat, dog, bird, etc.—with this newfound income. I always advise against this in the strongest terms possible. I cannot believe the amount of time Fluffy steals from her owners even during business hours (not even considering the amount of time Fluffy would steal from you while preparing for the CPA exams outside of work). You may be required to travel for work frequently, and Fluffy will only make your life more complicated. Not having a pet during my first two years in the industry gave me a leg up and allowed me to fully focus on my job and the CPA exams without being distracted by Fluffy back home. If Fluffy is just too cute to resist, promise yourself that you will only buy Fluffy once you have passed all CPA exams and turn the acquisition of Fluffy into a personal reward for a job well done.

The Sarbanes-Oxley Act (SOX) changed how the public accounting game is played dramatically. For example, the main way I have seen SOX impact the audit associate level is through the amount of time many audit associates now spend understanding, testing, and documenting their clients' internal control structures. Unfortunately, most recent graduates come into the workforce with little to no understanding of internal controls—they simply are not covered in depth at many colleges and universities in the U.S. One way academia could fine-tune its teaching to better prepare accounting students for the real world is by offering more classes on internal control structures and strategies. If you are entering an audit or advisory practice, you should brush up on internal controls before your first day at work. Thanks to SOX, many audit associates now spend massive amounts of time auditing these systems in addition to financial statement balances. You might want to ask each firm you interview with about the amount of time you could expect to spend testing and documenting internal controls. If you can get a clear answer, I would definitely keep this in mind as you evaluate firms. You may like working with internal controls or you may find that internal controls do not interest you. Either way, the amount of time you will spend on internal controls at each prospective firm should be something to marinate on during your interview process.

When you ultimately decide to move on from your firm (if ever), you will be remembered just as much for how you departed as for how you performed during your employment. Don't treat your final weeks like the second semester of your senior year of high school. Give at least two weeks notice, thank your firm for the opportunity, and try to leave on great terms with each of your coworkers. When you turn in your termination notice, be prepared for your firm to tell you that it does not need two weeks from you and would prefer that you terminate your employment immediately. Also, even if you despise one of your coworkers, in the long run it is not in your best interest to burn a bridge with anyone before or after you have officially departed. You may decide you want to come back to the firm or need the relationship down the road. After you turn in your notice, don't take your foot off the gas just because your plan is to move on to a different opportunity. Life is constantly changing, and you never know what the future may hold. One of my former coworkers worked as hard as anyone in the office during his last two weeks after he turned in his notice. He arrived early each morning, stayed late each evening, and was able to put the bow tie on a project we were working on together before he left for another opportunity. Everyone in the office took note of his work ethic during this period, and he left our firm on amazing terms. You should try to emulate this behavior. Although it may be tempting to slack off during your final weeks, if you keep your foot on the gas and finish strong you can put an exclamation point on a great career.

BLOCKCHAIN TECHNOLOGY

Many accountants (especially auditors) are worried blockchain technology may one day force them out of their careers in accounting. As much as the financial and technological communities hype the benefits of blockchain, its roll-out and widespread adoption may not be good for public accountants in the coming decades. For those of you who are unfamiliar with it, think of the blockchain as a ledger that permanently records all of a user's transactions. When new data is entered into the ledger, an immutable chain of information is created. Blockchain's proponents often hype this immutability—any digital information stored in the chain cannot be edited or altered. The chain grows as new information is entered into it, and any information coded into the chain is theoretically recorded in the chain for the rest of time. Many public accountants worry that it will be easy for an external party (the auditor) to validate and review financial activity recorded using blockchain technology. The ease of this review will further commoditize audits and reduce audit fees, audit firm size, and the overall need for auditors. Put simply, the fear is that there may not be a need for a large, technically proficient audit team to conduct a proper audit of a client on blockchain technology. Instead, one or two seasoned auditors could conduct the entire audit in a fraction of the previous time commitment by reviewing the financial activity and ending account balances found in the blockchain. It is not difficult to determine what this might mean for auditor job security, especially at the lower levels of the firm hierarchy.

Although the previous paragraph may sound frightening, my opinion is that accounting and blockchain are years away from marriage and effective widespread adoption. You will probably find that many of your clients run into problems using relatively standard accounting software. Blockchain technology will not eliminate the need for professional skepticism either. Even if blockchain technology becomes widely adopted, auditors should still have questions regarding how information is entered into the chain, whether the information corresponds with client operations and activities, and how that information can be trusted even if it is immutable once in the ledger. These are just a few of the questions auditors will have to ask their clients using blockchain technology. The blockchain may eliminate some lower level roles in the coming decades, but the higher level technical proficiency, judgment, and financial reporting expertise should always be needed. If you are already in public accounting or planning to join a practice, I do not think you should lose any sleep over blockchain. It is not worth changing careers now solely due to the fear of blockchain's possible disruption in the industry. Instead, turn this potential disruptor into a potential windfall by learning about blockchain technology now so you have a better chance of capitalizing on it if a blockchain related opportunity presents itself to you in the future. By the time the technology is widely and effectively adopted—if ever—you should already have progressed in your career to the point where you can leverage the technology to work for you.

CHAPTER 11

SETTING AND PURSUING GOALS

After you've found the right firm and you've structured your life correctly, the next biggest factor in your career success equation will be your goal setting. So many people in the U.S. go to work every day with zero goals in mind. They waffle and flounder year after year while mistakenly believing they are doing fine. Since they do not have a final destination in mind it is impossible to measure their progress. You should have goals around every aspect of your life, including your career. If you do not make a plan for your life, some other person is going to make it for you. This person will probably not have your best interest in mind. Many people are scared to set goals and exert significant energy in pursuit of their goals due to a paralyzing fear of what it would feel like to fall short after going all out in pursuit of their goals. This is a foolish way of thinking. Even if you do come up a little short of your goals, you will be better off than if you had not defined and aggressively pursued your goals. So go all out in every area of your life and in the pursuit of all of your goals. It sounds cheesy, but if you shoot for the moon and fall a little short, you will still end up with a mountain top view.

I was born and raised in Mississippi. I have never met anyone who had a better childhood than mine. I love the people in Mississippi and believe the state is the most underrated state in America. I recently moved back and do not plan to leave. However, the biggest flaw I find in the state is that it is not cool to try hard here. It's OK to sit back, be chill, and not "go all-in" on anything. After college I moved to Texas and slowly evolved into a Texan. Texans believe it is totally acceptable to put 100 percent effort into whatever it is that they are trying to accomplish. Whether you are working on an oil deal, a tech start-up, or a high school football career, in Texas it is completely acceptable to go all-in and be proud of your results. Texans believe they should be number one in every category. If they are not number one, they are ready to go down swinging in order to get there. They bet big and win big. When they strike out, they come right back to the plate as if the previous strike out didn't occur. This aggressive, fearless, and proud mentality is probably the biggest reason why the state is so successful and has become so wealthy. You will hear many Texans chanting "God Bless Texas" at sporting events and on any other occasion they deem appropriate. Unfortunately, many Mississippians would never even think of saying that about their state. The state has been so beaten down over the years that a discouragingly large percentage of people here have lost all sense of pride, self-confidence, and initiative. This negative mindset has led to an absence of widespread success across the state. Texas enjoys an abundance mentality, while Mississippi suffers from a scarcity mentality. Granted, in some instances the pride in Texas can lead to the occasional loud-talking, blow-hard reputation that so many outsiders complain about, and Mississippi's chill, laid-back personality leaves many first-time visitors talking about the "nice people" in Mississippi. I say all this to emphasize that you should approach your professional career with a Texas mentality, not a Mississippi mentality. Public accounting may not be the sexiest job on the planet, but if it is what you have chosen to spend any amount of your valuable life working on then you should go all-in without the fear of failure or of what other people might think or say about you once you start to push yourself.

You should accept the fact that there will always be jealous naysayers who discourage you from reaching for new heights as simply a fundamental truth about life. Members of this nasty group will never be genuinely excited about anyone else's attempt at real success because they have settled for mediocrity and are living far below their potential. Deep down they are terrified that you might actually find the success they could have if only they conquered their fear of taking action. On the other hand, there are plenty of genuine ballers out there who actually have achieved major accomplishments. Ironically, these people are often the most willing to support you in your attempt to do something exceptional because they are not intimidated by your success. They know that achieving tough goals is possible because they have already found great success, so they would never tell you that "it can't be done." As an example, many weak and out of shape people are afraid of joining a gym due to a fear of what the experienced and fit members of the gym might think about them. However, the fit members of the gym will actually be the last people to laugh at any out of shape newcomer. Those who have been working out for a long time understand that they too were once the new, physically unfit person in the gym. The newcomer will remind them of themselves. These people will surprisingly often go out of their way to support newcomers at the gym. Others can offer their opinions, and you should often listen to the opinions of people you trust, but only you have the right to define your life's potential. Don't let any jealous naysayers prevent you from pursuing the life you desire.

You should have major but specifically defined goals in every area of your life. For example, personal goals, career goals, and relationship goals are all necessary. Once you start setting goals you will quickly see how much more progress you make in life. I did not always harness this goal-setting phenomenon to my advantage. For many years I lived without specific, clearly defined goals in mind. As soon as I started setting clear goals and giving myself hard deadlines I found that progress and success seemed to accelerate towards me with intense speed. Now I have all sorts of goals. Personal goals, financial goals, and even goals related to life events such as buying my first house or taking a big vacation. I also have smaller goals within my major goals to help me track my progress in my month to month, week to week, and day to day existence. I have goals regarding the number of times I want to be able to bench press 225 pounds in one sitting by the end of the year, the number of copies of this book I want to sell, and goals related to when I want to arrive at work each morning. I like to set the bar ridiculously high so that the goals are remotely possible but not likely to be achieved. With a more difficult goal in mind, I have learned that my body and mind will adapt and make much more progress towards the higher goal than they would have made if I had set a lower bar. The life I desire to build becomes much more likely to manifest with the tougher goals in existence. The trick to avoid discouragement when you fail to reach a high bar is to prevent yourself from mentally labeling any of your

SETTING AND PURSUING GOALS

shortcomings as failures. Instead, view any shortcomings as harmless outcomes or even as assets that you now have the opportunity to use to your advantage. Even if you fall a little short of a super high bar, you will still be very happy with where you end up.

You want your goals in line with each other so that your life becomes one synchronized, well-oiled machine. You should not be setting goals for your mile run time while simultaneously setting goals over how quickly you can eat an extra-large cheese pizza. When your goals outside of your career are synchronized with your career goals, you will find that success at work comes to you with ease. Once you have your work goals in mind, write them down and tell the people in your inner circle about them. Do not worry about what these people might think of them—your goals are for your life not theirs. These actions will increase your chances of attainment significantly.

As a new hire fresh out of school, you should set two short-term to intermediate career goals right off the bat:

1 To pass all of the CPA exams as an associate
2 To make senior associate in the standard amount of time it takes to reach senior at your firm

Your firm may assign you an office mentor or coach. I was lucky enough to have fantastic company assigned coaches throughout my career. If your firm doesn't assign a mentor to you, ask a senior level co-worker to be your mentor. Tell this person your goals, ask if they seem realistic (they are), and ask this person to hold you accountable. The fact that you're reading this book tells me these goals are definitely within your potential striking distance. If you already had some accounting experience prior to joining your new firm, consider setting a goal to make senior in a shorter amount of time than it usually takes new hires straight out of school. Attaining these goals will be a serious challenge but definitely worth the reward in the long run. Thousands of people across the U.S. attain these goals each year, so you can too. As you make these goals, create rewards for yourself for the accomplishment of each goal. For example, after this book is written I plan on adopting a dog. Maybe once you obtain senior and/or the CPA you can reward yourself with a new car, a trip, a dinner at a Brazilian steakhouse, or a new toy you've always wanted. These rewards will give you something to look forward to outside of the face value benefit of obtaining the goal and will keep you motivated through the times when you feel like giving up or lack the motivation to keep pushing.

Maybe you realize that public accounting is definitely not the career for you after a year in the trenches. This is completely fine. Your goals should evolve as your life progresses, and in the future you may decide you would prefer to reach a different target instead of your original goal. This is all part of the process. Even if circumstances change and your old goals are no longer attainable, you will still find yourself in a great position to take advantage of new opportunities which otherwise wouldn't have been available without the progress made in your attempt to reach your initial goals. Whether you decide to stay in public accounting or not, you should make a goal to pass all of the CPA exams before you are promoted to senior associate. The next chapter is entirely dedicated to preparing for the CPA exams.

CHAPTER 12

STUDYING FOR THE CPA EXAMS

The CPA is mandatory if you decide to make a career out of public accounting. The industry is simply not worth the grind without the certification. It's safe to assume that you will not be promoted to manager at any firm until you obtain your CPA. I will admit I have heard of the non-CPA who is promoted to senior at a public accounting firm, switches into industry, and then works his way up the accounting ladder in industry without the CPA. But this is very rare, and I would guess 1 out of 100 non-CPAs can work their way up the accounting/finance ladder in this way. Commit this very moment to passing all of the CPA exams as an associate. If you are in a five year undergrad/masters program, make it a priority to pass all of the CPA exams while still in school or before you start work. Also, seriously consider delaying your firm start date to give you more time to study without the stress and time demands of work hanging over you. It might only take you a few months to pass all the exams if you are still in school or if you're taking a few months off before your start date. However, once you begin working it will probably take you much longer to pass all the exams. Everyone will tell you that it is many times more difficult to pass the CPA exams once you begin working full-time.

Don't make the mistake of waiting until you are promoted to senior to begin studying for the CPA exams. The senior level is widely considered to be much more stressful and time demanding than the associate level. You will just make it that much harder on yourself by waiting. In my opinion, your chances of passing the CPA exams drop like a rock if you attain the senior associate level without the CPA. You do not want to be the senior who is forever stuck at senior because you do not have the CPA. Not having it will also limit your options if you decide to leave public accounting without it. You will have to talk your way around not having it during interviews for other jobs and life will just become that much harder.

Below are some study tips and motivational encouragement that I used when I studied for the exams.

PRACTICAL STUDY TIPS AND ADVICE

I set a goal to review every potential exam topic two weeks before each of my scheduled exam dates. After working through all the potential exam topics, I would take a practice test. During each practice test I would write down every question or topic that seemed particularly challenging or unfamiliar to me. This list would become a databank of unfamiliar and challenging topics and questions which I would study immediately after taking the practice test and again in the days leading up to the actual exam. In my opinion the toughest aspect of the exams was simply the volume of material each exam covers. It can be difficult to decide which portions of the study material to focus on during your final review in the days leading up to each exam. This databank method pinpoints the exam topics you should devote your limited energy toward as the exam date approaches. When studying for tests and exams in college, I discovered I had a bad habit of studying the test material I knew well while subconsciously avoiding and blocking out unfamiliar material. The beauty of this databank method is that it does not permit you to engage in that kind of costly behavior.

I took all four CPA exams while working full-time. I liked to schedule my CPA exams on Mondays and take the prior Fridays off. If you can afford to take more vacation days off, it would be well worth it to use as many as you think you might need to adequately prepare. In the long run, burning vacation time for each exam is worth the short-term sacrifice. Taking Friday off before each exam gave me the Thursday night through that Monday morning to review for the Monday exam without being distracted by work. As an additional bonus, if your firm learns you used your vacation day to study, your reputation as someone who cares about the job and your career will further develop.

Schedule the exam you think will require the least amount of study during the time of year in which it will be the most difficult to study. You don't want to find yourself studying for the toughest exam in the middle of your firm's busy season or during the summer when you're scheduled to travel to all ten of your best friends' weddings.

Find a place to live that is close to your office—or client, if you will be frequently working from a specific client's office—even if it means paying a premium. I lived one mile away from my firm's office as an associate. The time I saved by living so close to work gave me hours of extra time each day. An extra hour or two of free time each weekday is worth at least a couple hundred dollars a month, even if you aren't always using the time to study.

Use colored note cards as flash cards when studying. You can buy packs of hundreds of red, green, yellow, blue, and orange flash cards for a few dollars at most convenience stores. If you buy 3' by 5' cards, cut them in half so you have double the inventory. Keep these cards nearby while you work through your study material. Each time you come across a word, principle, or list that you need to memorize, write it down on one side of the card and write the meaning or definition of the term on the other. Write down the next term on a different colored card. Continue this process until you have exhausted all of your colors, and then repeat with your first color. My mind's ability to retain information skyrockets when I use colored flash cards. I learned this trick in college while my college roommate was taking German classes (thanks, Patrick). He could memorize the meanings of hundreds of German words each night with these colored flash cards, so I decided to give them a shot during my senior year of college. I could not have been more pleased with the results. Colored flash cards probably boosted my college GPA that semester by 0.5 points and were instrumental in giving me the ability to pass all of the CPA exams on my first attempt while working full-time.

If you are lacking the motivation to study, try studying with a lit scented candle nearby—if safe and legal to do so. I discovered that scented candles helped me focus during my senior year of college. At one point during the year I decided to study with a scented candle burning nearby. After a few weeks of studying with a scented candle burning, whenever I smelled the scent of the candle I would naturally want to crack open a textbook and begin reading. My subconscious had associated the pleasant smell of the candle with studying. In the real world I used the same tactic to motivate myself to study in the evenings after long days at work. Similar to Pavlov's famous dog, whenever I smelled the scent of the burning candle after work my motivation to study suddenly appeared. I actually brought this tactic back out of my toolbox while writing this book. I will readily admit the scented candle trick sounds exceedingly quirky, but it works for me and should work for you as well.

Keep a clean and organized desk to help you retain the information you learn in your studies. You are more likely to feel the desire to study at an organized desk than at an unorganized and messy desk. Our physical environments impact our mental clarity and thought processes much more than most people realize. I found that if I studied at a clean and organized desk, my brain was much more likely to keep any information learned organized and accessible in my mind. If I studied at an unorganized and messy desk, the information I learned was likely to be unorganized, messy, and less accessible in my brain. Many people have told me they have observed the same phenomenon, so this is definitely something that you should keep in mind as you study.

Physically remove your distractions. Throw away your video games, cut your cable, and put down the beer (or anything else that could be a major distraction). I have heard too many young public accountants talk about partying, playing video games, or watching TV for hours each night after work instead of studying for their exams. Reward yourself with a new console using the bonus money you receive for passing the exams. The CPA will give you dozens of opportunities that your video games will not. High school and college was the time for partying, binge watching TV shows, and playing video games. Now is the time for passing the CPA exams, working hard, and making money. You probably will not even be able to enjoy your distractions with the lingering feeling deep down inside you telling you that you really should be studying. Obtaining the CPA is not an indomitable task. It will take months of hard work, but keep reminding yourself that once you obtain the CPA you will have an amazing salary headed your way each year for the rest of your life and a broader path to new opportunities. If you do not think the CPA is for you, you probably want to start looking for another career. It simply does not make sense to be in public accounting without the CPA.

Social media is so time consuming for some that it warrants its own paragraph. If social media is distracting you from studying, delete it. Deleting it may not feel good in the short term, but your future self will thank you profusely. If you are not strong enough to totally delete it, give yourself only one day a week to view it. The majority of posts are on Sunday anyway. If you delete or severely limit your use of social media then your ability to focus and your mental storage space will expand immensely. You won't miss anything by only checking your accounts one day a week, and your mind will be much clearer. I have deleted several of my social media accounts in the past. Each time my mind felt like it was able to access another one hundred gigabytes of storage space that had previously been clogged up by photos of friends, their cats and dogs, and memes. Our brains were not designed to know what all of our friends are doing at any given moment. Seeing that information and retaining it in my brain took up way too much of my mental storage capacity, and I could not have been more thankful after I deleted my social media.

Obtaining the CPA will obviously require some sacrifices. One of these might revolve around the time you wake up each morning. You will probably have to wake up before 6:30 am each day to study while working full-time. This probably will mean heading to bed around 10:00 pm each night if you want to keep functioning at a high level for a long period of time. Don't waste time before or after work by playing on your phone or surfing the web. If your smart phone is too distracting, buy an old-school flip phone for this season of life. Also, try to exercise multiple times each week. If you are physically blessed with the capacity to do so, you should always carve out the time to exercise no matter how busy you are. If you don't have access to a gym, you can get a great workout by doing push-ups, sit-ups, body squats, and planks—you can even do these comfortably in a hotel room. You may find that you retain information better if you study while your mind is fresh in the morning instead of in the evening after a long, challenging day at the office. The evening may be a better time for you to blow off steam and stress with a workout. Whether you decide to exercise before or after work, your mental facilities will become stronger due to the extra energy your physical work-outs give you each week.

Once you begin working you will hear many associates and interns complain about the lack of time available to study for the exams after work. There can be merit to this point, so you need to find ways to save time. One way to save time is through your eating habits and meal selection. If you work late into the evening—after 8:30 pm, for example—your firm may order dinner for you. If you can afford it, drive-through and take-out options are always great. Meal delivery to your home would probably be efficient as well. If you live alone, you will probably find that cooking for one can be more expensive and time consuming than going out. I do not recommend cooking meals for yourself if you are studying for the exams, but if you must cook at home try to cook meals that do not require much preparation. Keep this mealtime commitment in mind when you are shopping for food.

Buying a rice cooker was one of the best investments I ever made. Discovering pre-marinated meats at my local grocery store was another huge win. I can put together tasty and nutritious chicken, rice, and veggie dishes in a matter of minutes with these items. You may not like the sound of this meal, but there are definitely ways for you to quickly and efficiently cook the meals you enjoy without taking up too much of your valuable study time.

MOTIVATION

Feel free to reference the motivational snippets below whenever you feel the need. The discussions below are basically paraphrases of separate conversations I have had with younger friends who were beginning to study for the CPA exams or were losing motivation to keep studying. I've listed some common excuses and difficulties as well as my talking points around each obstacle. Each of my responses was so well received by my friends that I felt the need to include our discussions here for your benefit.

"Now is just not the right time for me to begin studying"

There will always be an excuse not to study for the exams. Busy season, the summer, football season, and the holidays are all excuses public accountants will use to convince themselves that now is not the right time to begin studying. To be honest, the time to begin studying is never going to be perfect, so if you are waiting for the perfect time you will never actually begin studying. If you find that your firm demands so much of your time that you honestly don't have time to study outside of work, you should talk to someone at your firm about creating a fixed work schedule that will give you time to study outside of work once you have put a set amount of work hours in each week. If your firm does not want to work with you to come up with a reasonable work schedule, it may be worth considering a change to a firm with a better work-life balance. At the time of this writing, firms all over the country are desperate to hire associates and seniors. I am all for putting in the long hours at your firm, especially in your Trial Phase, but you also have to remember to look out for number one. It is your career and livelihood on the line, not your firm's. In the long run the CPA is more important and will boost your career earnings far more than the extra 10-20 hours a week your firm might want you to spend working rather than studying. Your firm will also benefit from having another licensed CPA on its staff.

"I always get distracted by work when I try to study"

When it's time to study don't let your mind wander back to worrying about work. Shut down your email and turn off your phone. Worry about work during the workday, but set a clear mental boundary so that you can focus on studying when you are not at work. You won't be billing hours for the time at home spent worrying about work. Don't take work home with you in your head—leave work at work and fully dedicate your time outside of work to studying.

"I've been studying hard, but I just don't feel prepared to schedule an exam"

If you are feeling like the chances of actually taking an exam are diminishing by the day, you might try scheduling an exam for a month or two out from today even if you are not 100 percent sure that you will have given yourself enough time to fully prepare. Once the exam is scheduled, your mind is more likely to find the motivation to study. This strategy of going all-in on a task is known as "burning your ships." This term originates in ancient times when armies would sink their ships after landing in hostile territory to eliminate the option of retreat. They were forced to win the impending battle or die trying, which would greatly increase their odds of winning. This theory also works in reverse. Ancient armies sometimes would only attack a city from three sides, leaving the fourth side open for the city's defenders to retreat. With the option to retreat now lingering in the back of the defending soldiers' minds, they were less likely to go all-in on defending the city. In theory, if the attacking army completely surrounded the city, the defenders would commit their last ounce of physical and mental energy to fighting off the attacking army since there was no chance for escape. If you continue telling yourself that you need to feel more prepared before you schedule your exam, you may never actually schedule it. Obviously, there is a fine line between this strategy and recklessness, but if you find yourself slipping into a motivation-less downward spiral, scheduling an exam today could be exactly what is needed to put you back on the right track. Keep in mind though that failed exams cannot immediately be retaken, and there are limited months in which applicants can even take the exams. Don't be reckless, but burning your ships may be the perfect remedy for your lack of motivation.

"Another person's event is happening that I can't afford to miss, so I can't study"

Don't squander your life watching another guy live his dream, make millions of dollars, and get the girl while you sit on your couch. Don't throw your life away living vicariously through another person, thinking that another person's achievements will validate you, or chasing another person's goals for your life. You should be the main character in your life story. Sadly, I meet so many people who would not even be the main character if a movie was made about their lives. These people are more concerned with other people's achievements on the athletic field, in entertainment, or in politics than they are with their own goals and problems. I am all for placing others ahead of yourself in your day-to-day interactions and abiding by the Golden Rule, but make sure that you would be the main character if a movie was made about your life.

"But my favorite team is playing, and these guys are doing something real"

If you are studying during a time when your favorite team is playing its biggest games, give yourself permission to watch one game each weekend. After the game is over, go back to your desk and keep studying. It may feel good in the short run to watch sports all weekend, but you can't afford to waste this precious study time. It will feel extremely painful in the long run if you do not get the CPA. Passing the exams is not exactly signing a million dollar contract, but the CPA does give you massive career earnings potential over a forty or fifty year career. The average NFL player makes amazing money, but only for three years. With the CPA you have the chance to make great money for forty years or more. At a certain point in your accounting career you might command a higher salary than many professional athletes. In addition to limiting the number of games you watch each week, cut out watching any time-sucking TV anchors and talking heads. I love sports more than anybody, but spending time watching talking heads debate who the greatest NBA player is, how high a college athlete's draft status might have risen or fallen, or which team has the best chance of winning next year's World Series is an UTTER WASTE OF TIME. These predictions rarely, if ever, come true, and you don't gain anything even on the off chance a talking head is correct. Make your life a priority and do not get caught up in that garbage. You get one ride on this roller coaster, so make the most of it while you are on it.

CHAPTER 13

THE CFE AND OTHER CERTIFICATIONS

In addition to the CPA, there are several other certifications and designations you may want to consider. I primarily want to discuss the Certified Fraud Examiner (CFE) in this chapter, since I possess the CFE certification. However, do not even read this chapter if you do not have the CPA yet. In my opinion the CFE and all other designations and certifications are fantastic, but nothing will open as many doors in public accounting as the CPA. This chapter is for CPA eyes only. For those who do not have the CPA yet, knock out the CPA first and then come back to this chapter. If you are in tax, financial statement audit, or advisory then you need to have your CPA to be promoted to manager and open doors to outside positions, not the CFE or any other credential. The CFE and other certifications and designations may be more important than the CPA in other lines of work, but in public accounting the CPA is the ice cream, the chocolate sauce, the bananas, the whipped cream, and the nuts. Any other certification or designation is a cherry on top. To repeat: do not waste your valuable time reading this chapter if you do not have the CPA.

For the readers who already have the CPA: I decided to study for the CFE during my second year as an associate. The second year associate has advantages: you begin to put the pieces of the puzzle together, but you still are not under as much pressure or have as much responsibility as you will have as a first year senior associate. I had settled into a pretty good rhythm at the end of my second busy season. I was able to do what I needed to do at work and leave around 6:00 pm each day that spring. Although work was going well, I unfortunately found myself heading home after work and twiddling my thumbs for hours each night before going to sleep and doing it all over again the next day.

One day that spring I was conducting one of my firm's standard tests to check for fraud and I was hit with a frightening realization. I didn't feel very confident that I would be able to detect fraudulent activity even if the numbers were screaming "FRAUD" at me in the testing. If you feel the same way now, the CFE might be good for you. I thought about how pathetic and awkward it would be to let a massive fraud go undetected at one of our clients or in any future business deals in which I participated. I assumed there were probably dozens of fraud schemes for bad actors to put into action that I didn't even know existed. After several more nights of going home after work and wasting the evenings, I knew it was best for me in the long run to use this time to begin preparing for the CFE exams instead of wasting my time away.

After I committed to take the exams, I conducted some preliminary reconnaissance on the CFE and learned some startling information. I learned some surveys have found that "organizations around the world

THE CFE AND OTHER CERTIFICATIONS

lose an estimated five percent of their annual revenues due to fraud."[4] I thought this five percent figure was outrageous, as some companies can only hope to make one cent in profit for every dollar of revenue, if they are even profitable at all. This finding aroused my intrigue in the world of fraud detection, as its effects were obviously much more rampant than I had initially realized. I also learned that the CFE is widely considered to be one of the most recession-proof certifications in America. Fraud typically spikes during recessions as company sales quotas and profitability goals become harder to realize without cutting corners, and thus the demand for CFEs actually surges upward during economic downturns. I learned this in May of 2019, over twelve years since the beginning of the last financial crisis in 2007. The Trump economy was on fire, but I had always heard that recessions can usually be expected to occur every four to eight years. It appeared we were overdue. The next recession seemed like it would be even nastier than 2008. Higher household, corporate, and national debt levels, a Federal Reserve with even less room to cut interest rates, and a baby boomer pension crisis all worried me. Instead of fretting over these circumstances, I decided it was in my best interest to take action to further recession-proof my résumé by getting the CFE.

The CFE is not just for accountants, but there is some overlap in the material covered on the CFE and the CPA. In my opinion you could have an advantage over non-CPAs due to your accounting background. I put my unfamiliar topics listing method to good use again while studying for the CFE. I wrote down every term or phrase that seemed unfamiliar on the practice tests and focused on that information immediately after the practice tests and in the days leading up to

---

4   https://www.acfe.com/press-release.aspx?id=4294973129

each exam. This technique worked for me yet again, just as it did in college and in my preparation for the CPA. I was able to knock out the CFE exams several months after I made the initial commitment to study for them. I am sure you can do the same if you will commit to putting the time in.

There are several other certifications and designations that many public accountants will pursue. These include the Certified Internal Auditor (CIA), the Certified Information Systems Auditor (CISA), the Certified Valuation Analyst (CVA), and several others. Adding a second set of letters to the alphabet soup at the end of your name can only benefit you. I doubt the average bystander knows what any accounting related certification stands for, yet the perception the second set of letters creates can blow people away, especially if you are young and only beginning your career. In fact, I bet seeing the CFE behind my name on the cover of this book may have given many of you the extra nudge you needed to follow through with the purchase. However, make sure you have gotten the hang of work and are easily hitting your hours targets before you begin an outside project like studying for a second certification. But if you find yourself wasting time after work each night and are looking for the next project to undertake, another designation or certification may be exactly what you need to continue to develop yourself and add another skill-set to your professional toolbox.

I hope you will be able to use the workplace cheat codes and career advice found in this section to your advantage. Now it is time to move on to our fourth and final section of the book. In this section we will dive into the words, phrases, and abbreviations that you need to know in order to experience success as a new hire.

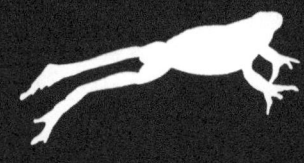

SECTION 4

GLOSSARY AND FAREWELL

GLOSSARY

LINGO YOU DIDN'T HEAR IN SCHOOL

I want to give you a glossary of widely used accounting terms, phrases, and abbreviations that accounting students rarely or never hear in school. Working to accomplish a task before I knew the meanings of these terms was like attempting to reach the end of an arduous journey without the ability to read the map. I spent more time straining to decipher the map legend than actually undertaking the journey. This led to incredible frustration and wasted time. During the midst of a hectic project the last place you want to find yourself is scrambling for the meaning of important abbreviations or phrases related to the task at hand. Fortunately, as you will see below, you do not have to be a rocket scientist to grasp the meanings of these terms. Most are fairly straightforward or self-evident once you know the abbreviation or discover the meaning. Different firms and practice groups will probably have different names for many of these terms, but reviewing the definitions and examples below will still be beneficial no matter which firm or practice you join. I come from an audit background, so I will admit these terms and phrases could be slanted toward those going into an audit practice. However, these terms and definitions are so basic and widely used among the public accounting profession that even those going into tax or advisory practices need to know the meanings. I have learned that it is easy to grasp the definition of a term or idea once I see it in a sentence and/or see an example of the term in use, so I have shown generic and simple examples of these terms in use when practical to better illustrate their meanings. You may not be an expert on these terms and meanings after reading through this list, but skimming through this glossary will make things a little less confusing for you during your first few weeks at work.

As a side note, I would not use these terms or abbreviations at work unless other people at your firm already use them. When communicating with others, you want to make it as easy as possible for the recipient of your communication to grasp your message. Using a term or abbreviation that your recipient is not familiar with will only make your message more difficult to grasp. You will of course come across words and phrases while working that are not included in this glossary. Each time you come across a word or phrase that is unfamiliar to you, stop what you are doing, look it up, and write it down. Create your own databank of these words and phrases so you can leverage what you've learned in the future when needed.

409A Valuation: An appraisal of a private company's common stock value which is conducted by an independent valuation specialist. If a private company intends to issue stock options, it will need to obtain a 409A valuation in order to value the options and comply with

IRS regulations. Since public companies are publicly traded at readily discernible market values, 409A valuations are not needed by them. However, private companies need to use 409A Valuation specialists to value their stock options and protect stakeholders from IRS penalties and fees.

ACA: The Affordable Care Act

ACH Payment: ACH stands for Automated Clearing House. ACH's are digital payments that a financial institution will make at an account holder's request. You may be asked to gather confirmation of the ACH payment by obtaining a client's bank statements or ACH confirmation notification. Many students have no idea what ACH's are before they enter the business world as very few individuals make payments outside of cash, checks, or debit/credit cards. If you see ACH written somewhere, do not over analyze the meaning or become frightened by the unfamiliar term. ACH is just a term for another payment mechanism.

AFDA: Allowance for Doubtful Accounts.

AFS: Audited Financial Statements.

Agings: Documents created to lay out the "age" of all the components of a bigger balance. Agings usually separate balances into groupings called "buckets." You will frequently see Agings related to receivables and payables. Similar to details, schedules, and listings, the total account balances seen on Agings should tie out to the trial balance. Agings are generally easier to understand once you have seen an example, so I have provided an example AP aging below.

Workpaper 7000						
12/31/2019 AP Aging						
Vendor Name	Invoice Date	Invoice Total	0-30 Days	31-60 Days	61-90 Days	> 90 Days
Vendor A	12/15/2019	$1,250.00	$1,250.00			
Vendor B	12/10/2019	$15,000.00	$15,000.00			
Vendor C	11/20/2019	$7,000.00		$7,000.00		
Vendor D	10/14/2019	$2,500.00			$2,500.00	
Vendor E	7/15/2019	$900.00				$900.00
Totals		$26,650.00	$16,250.00	$7,000.00	$2,500.00	$900.00

Analytic: Analytics are calculations used to analyze data from one period against a previous period, industry standards, or some other benchmark. Analytics can provide new or additional insight into the financial statements and highlight any anomalies. Before conducting any analytic, your firm will probably ask you to come up with an expectation (similar to a hypothesis) based on your understanding of the client and activity during the period. You probably will also be tasked with understanding common analytics when studying for the CPA exams. AR Turnover, Days Sales in AR, Inventory Turnover, AP Turnover, and Gross Margin Percentages are some of the common, widely used analytics. For those going into audit or advisory, you should try to have at least a cursory understanding of the widely used analytics before your first day at work. As analytics can be unique to specific engagements, below is a simple Sales to Sales Commissions Paid analytic for you to see as an example.

Workpaper 3000				
2019 Sales Commission Analytic				
	2017	2018	2019	2018-2019 Variance
Sales	$50.00	$100.00	$150.00	
Sales Commission Paid	$5.00	$10.00	$30.00	
Percentage of Sales Paid As Commission	10.00%	10.00%	20.00%	10.00%

By reviewing the simple analytic above, the viewer can ascertain that sales commissions as a percentage of total sales increased by 10 percent from 2018 to 2019. By comparing this increase to the consistency in the percentage from 2017 to 2018, the viewer may be able to glean additional insight into financial activity during 2019. Seeing financial data presented in this manner will lead to enhanced decision-making abilities.

Articles of Incorporation: Official documents filed with a government entity to formalize the incorporation of a business.

The Binder: The documentation storage center your firm uses to store support. Your firm will probably store its documentation for many years after the issuance of any report or deliverable for liability purposes. In the past these storage centers consisted of physical binders, but most firms now store all documentation in electronic data centers.

The Board and Board Minutes: The shareholders of a company will usually put shareholder representatives on a governing committee called "The Board." Think of The Board as the boss of client management (although client management can be on The Board). Boards will usually have meetings multiple times a year to plan, monitor company performance, implement changes, and do anything necessary to run the company from the tip top. Board Minutes are the official records of Board meetings. These Board Minutes can provide a treasure trove of information that can be reviewed to gain an understanding of a client's activity during the year. All of the major activities that a company engages in will be discussed and monitored by The Board, so in theory a record of all major company activity should be mentioned in the company's Board Minutes. M&A activity, dividend determinations, debt raises, hirings, firings, new business lines, and many other important topics could be discussed in the Board Minutes.

BOL: Bill of Lading. A BOL is a receipt given by a carrier of a shipment of goods to the sender of the goods to confirm the nature, quantity, and destination of the goods being shipped.

BOM: Bill Of Materials. A BOM is a list of the materials or parts that are needed to manufacture a product.

CAPEX: Capital Expenditure. A Capital Expenditure is basically a sizable investment made by a company in hopes of generating a return on the investment at least a year into the future. For example, CAPEX can refer to the purchase of property, equipment, furniture, machinery, vehicles, or some other long-term investment. Try to think about "capitalization" (recording the purchase as an asset) when you hear the term CAPEX.

Cap Table: Capitalization Table. A Cap Table usually displays a company's equity distribution, equity types, and equity values used in each investment round.

Check Register: A Check Register is simply a file that lists all checks written from a certain account or group of accounts during a certain time period. Check Registers help accountants review cash disbursements.

Clerically Accurate: A Clerically Accurate page means there are no typos on the page and that all of the calculations on the page have been reperformed to check for any mathematical errors.

Confirm: Confirm is short for Confirmation. Auditors will frequently send Confirms to financial institutions, lenders, and shareholders to confirm client balances.

Coverage: The word "Coverage" usually means the tested portion of a total population of a balance. Suppose your client has a $100,000 accounts receivable balance. If your firm successfully confirms $90,000 of the $100,000 balance with your client's customers, then your firm could say it has obtained a 90 percent Coverage of the total accounts receivable balance. Auditors will often test a portion of a total account balance in order to gain comfort over the entire balance without having to test every last penny that composes the balance.

Credit Limit: The total amount of goods or services a business will permit a customer to buy on credit. If the credit limit has been met, the customer should be barred from buying anything else until cash has been collected from the customer and its outstanding balance has been paid down.

Credit Memo: Credit memo is short for Credit Memorandum. Credit Memos are common documents in American business. A credit memo is simply a document issued by a seller to formally reduce the amount owed to the seller by a buyer under the terms of a previous sales arrangement. The reduction can occur due to a return of goods previously purchased, dissatisfaction with the sale, a pricing disagreement, or buyer financial difficulty. Credit memos can support reductions in receivables/payables and the related revenue/expenses.

Cross-Foot: To Cross-Foot is to sum a row of numbers. It is just a sideways version of a foot (see below).

Workpaper 9500						
AR Aging						
Customer Name	0-30 Days	31-60 Days	61-90 Days	> 90 Days	Total	
Customer A	$10.00	$25.00	$15.00	$12.00	$62.00	Rx

If you summed the amounts in the four buckets above, you would have "cross-footed" the schedule. Your firm may have a designated tickmark to denote that a listing has been cross-footed. In this example I used the abbreviation "Rx" (short for "recalculated") to indicate that the four bucket totals had been added together to find the $62 total.

Cut-Off: Cut-off refers to your client's period end. For example, if a client has a December 31 year-end, then the literal cut-off is midnight on New Year's Eve. It is important that your client does not record entries in one period that should actually be booked in a different period. You will often hear the term being tossed around during the testing of inventory and revenue. Cut-off procedures refers to testing done to ensure amounts were booked in the proper period.

Debt Covenant: An agreement made by a lender and borrower in connection with the issuance of a loan. Often a lender will require that a borrower meet specific financial goals and refrain from certain activities while indebted. One reason this is done is to reduce the cost of borrowing. With its demands otherwise met, in theory a lender would be willing to lend at a lower interest rate. However, an insidious lender might use Debt Covenants to her advantage by structuring them so that the borrower is out of compliance as soon as the loan is issued. Debt Covenants will probably be found in your clients' debt agreements, so you will have to actually read the agreements to understand the covenants. There usually will be penalties involved if a debtor ever falls out of compliance with its Debt Covenants. Depending on the terms of the loan, if non-compliance is found to exist the creditor could demand immediate payment, increase the interest rate or collateral, or seek other recourse. As an external accountant you need to be concerned about this. For example, if a creditor can demand immediate payment of debt due to non-compliance, what was previously non-current debt might need to be reclassified as current debt. This reclassification could severely impact dozens of financial ratios and make the company less valuable in the eyes of outsiders. However, a creditor can also issue a waiver to forgive the sin of non-compliance. Long story short, if you ever are assigned to review a client's debt balances, you probably will need to be familiar with your client's Debt Covenants.

Detail Review: To Detail Review a work-paper is to literally re-perform the work conducted on a work-paper exactly how it was initially completed by the preparer. As the preparer, assume your first reviewer will be detail reviewing all of your work. Write, organize, and label your work so that you make it as easy as possible for your reviewer to re-perform the steps you took to complete the project.

Details, Schedules, and Listings: The inter-connectivity between Details, Schedules, and Listings (all three of these terms mean basically the same thing), the trial balance, and the financial statements gave me trouble as a new hire. Looking back I am pretty embarrassed about it because the terms "Detail," "Schedule," and "Listing" each refers to a simple report that breaks out a larger amount. For example, let's suppose a client has $500 in its prepaid insurance account. A Detail of that account is a report that shows the "details" of the entries that compose the account's ending $500 balance. The specific data shown in these reports can vary depending on the accounting system that generates the report. These reports could list the journal entry number, the account class, the amount of the debit/credit, the date of the entry, the supplier/vendor, the creator of the entry, as well as other information. These reports can often be created/filtered by customer, by vendor, by user, by amount, and by date.

Usually Details, Schedules, and Listings will show the details or break outs of trial balance account balances. Trial balance accounts compose the financial statements. Think of Details, Schedules, and Listings as zoomed in pictures that drill down into financial statement account balances at a granular level. All Details, Schedules, and Listings should tie out to the client trial balance in one way or another.

LINGO YOU DIDN'T HEAR IN SCHOOL

See the example below for an illustration of how Details, Schedules, and Listings should agree to the trial balance and how the trial balance should tie into the financial statements.

Workpaper 1220
December 31, 2019 Prepaid Insurance Detail

Name	Date	Vendor	Amount	
Prepaid Insurance #1	12/22/2019	Insurance Company A	$100.00	
Prepaid Insurance #2	12/24/2019	Insurance Company B	$125.00	
Prepaid Insurance #3	12/26/2019	Insurance Company C	$130.00	
Prepaid Insurance #4	12/28/2019	Insurance Company D	$145.00	
Total Prepaid Insurance - Account 3100			$500.00	1100

Workpaper 1100
December 31, 2019 Trial Balance - Prepaid Expenses

Account Number	Account Name	Account Balance	
3000	Prepaid Rent	$100.00	
3100	Prepaid Insurance	$500.00	1220
3200	Prepaid Utilities	$50.00	
3300	Prepaid Marketing	$125.00	
Total Prepaid Expenses		$775.00	5000

Workpaper 5000
Financial Statements

Assets			
Cash		$125.00	
Accounts Receivable		$200.00	
Prepaid Expenses		$775.00	1100
Fixed Assets		$1,000.00	
Total Assets		$2,100.00	

In the example above, the company has four prepaid expense accounts: rent, insurance, utilities, and marketing. You can see these four accounts in the trial balance at work-paper 1100. In work-paper

1220, I created an example prepaid insurance detail which shows the break out of the $500 prepaid insurance balance. By following the tie outs you can see how the $500 total prepaid insurance balance from the prepaid insurance detail agrees to the trial balance, and how the $775 total prepaid balance from the trial balance agrees to the financial statements. Accounts do not necessarily have to be split out into as much detail as the four separate prepaid accounts above. Depending on the preferences of the company, a major financial statement account balance could only have one related account number.

Disbursement Listing: A Disbursement Listing is simply a list of all cash disbursements made by a company during a given time period.

EBP: Employee Benefit Plan.

EIN: Employer Identification Number.

EL: Engagement Letter. An EL spells out the terms and details of the engagement. It should be signed by the client, preferably before any work in the engagement is undertaken. You may or may not have any interaction with EL's as an associate or intern, but it will be a good abbreviation to know regardless.

Fidelity Bond: A Fidelity Bond is basically an insurance policy that reimburses policyholders for losses incurred as a result of fraudulent or dishonest acts by certain individuals.

Fieldwork: Fieldwork is the phase of an engagement traditionally performed "in the field" (usually at a client site). It is the evidence

LINGO YOU DIDN'T HEAR IN SCHOOL

gathering, evaluation, and documentation phase of the engagement. It usually follows the Planning phase and precedes the Reporting or Wrap Up phase of the engagement. I think of Fieldwork as the meat and potatoes phase. As a new associate or intern, you will probably spend most of your time completing the Fieldwork phase while your superiors work on the Planning and Wrap Up phases.

Flux: Flux is short for "fluctuation." This is another elementary term that (embarrassingly) scared me when I first heard it in use. Fortunately, to Flux an account is only to compare it against the same balance from a prior period to visualize how the balance changed from one period to the next. You can express a Flux in dollar and/or in percentage terms to show how the balance increased or decreased from period 1 to 2. Below is a screenshot of a Flux for further clarification.

Workpaper 2000					
2019 Accounts Receivable Flux					
Account Number	Account Name	2018 Balance	2019 Balance	$ Variance	% Variance
1500	Accounts Receivable	$100.00	$200.00	$100.00	100.00%
1550	Allowance for Doubtful Accounts	$5.00	$7.00	$2.00	40.00%

FOB Destination: FOB Destination stands for Free on Board Destination. This is a shipping term that indicates the buyer takes possession of the shipment as soon as the shipment reaches the shipping destination. This timing can impact a multitude of financial statement accounts.

FOB Shipping Point: Free on Board Shipping Point. This term is similar to FOB Destination. It is a shipping term that indicates the buyer takes possession of the shipment as soon as the shipment departs from the shipping point.

Foot: To Foot is to sum a column of numbers. Do not over-think Footing—it isn't hard.

Workpaper 9000		
Sales By Customer		
Customer A	$100.00	
Customer B	$125.00	
Customer C	$60.00	
Customer D	$30.00	
Total	$315.00	Rx

If you summed the sales shown in the listing above, you would have "footed" the schedule. Your firm may have a designated tick-mark used to denote that a listing has been footed. In this example I used the abbreviation "Rx" to indicate that all four sales amounts had been added together to find the $315 total.

Form 5500: A Form 5500 is an annual report filed with the U.S. Department of Labor by an employee benefit plan sponsor (if you were ever a participant in a 401(k) plan sponsored by your employer, your employer sponsoring the plan was the plan sponsor) that provides regulators with information regarding the plan's financial health and plan investment and operational information.

Form W-2: A U.S. government tax form used by employers to report wages paid to each employee and the tax withholdings related to each employee's wages. W-2s are issued by a company to its employees and copies are filed with the government. As an employee, you will need to use your W-2 to do your taxes each year. Keep in mind that independent contractors should not receive Form W-2s, only employees receive W-2s from their employers.

Form W-3: A U.S. government tax form used by employers to report the total earnings, Medicare wages, and Social Security wages of all of its employees to the government. W-3s are not required to be sent to individual employees, only the government.

GL: General Ledger.

I-9: Forms all new U.S. employees are required to fill out for identity and employment authorization purposes. On your first day of work you will probably be asked to fill out an I-9.

IA: Internal Audit.

Invoice: An invoice is a document sent by a seller to a buyer to formalize a sale and notify the buyer of how much is owed to the seller on account of the sale. The seller's invoice may contain much of the same information as the buyer's PO. An invoice can be sent before, alongside, or after the services or goods are delivered to the buyer. Invoices can contain the transaction date, the transaction amount, the quantities and types of goods or services ordered, payment terms, and other information related to the sale as well.

IPE: Information Produced by the Entity. The accuracy and trustworthiness of IPE is something external accountants must constantly wrestle with. Using IPE is a balancing act. Your firm should have standard policies and procedures to guide you through your use of all IPE.

ITGC: Information Technology General Controls. These are the controls surrounding the IT side of a company's control structure.

MRL: Management Representation Letter.

One-Off: A One-off is a freak, one-time occurrence that is not expected to be repeated. Clients or members of your firm might refer to an occurrence as a "one-off" event.

Open For: The phrase "Open For" stands for the items that have yet to be completed or received. For example, if you are talking with your senior about the support requested but not yet received from the client, you might say "we have received all asset and expense details, but we are still open for the payroll rec support."

Open Item List: A list of all items requested of the client by your engagement team that have not been provided to date. It is important to stay on top of the Open Item List and to know which items on the list are highest priority. If your client tells you that he only has time to send over two or three items or pieces of support, it is great if you can quickly tell him the highest priority items needed to keep the engagement progressing smoothly.

OPEX: Operating Expenditure. An Operating Expenditure is made by a company in hopes of utilizing the benefit of the expenditure in the current year. These are the day-to-day expenses that keep the company functioning on a daily basis. OPEX can include Selling, General,

Administrative, Payroll, Sales Commissions, and Travel fees. Think of short-term benefits whenever you hear the term OPEX.

Packing List: A shipping document that lists the items and materials included within a specific shipment. These lists can include the types, quantities, descriptions, and/or carrying weights of the items included within the shipment. A Packing List will help a buyer check to ensure that the contents of the shipment matches his previous order. Packing Lists can also be referred to as Packing Slips.

Payroll Providers: Companies that help other companies process their payrolls. Payroll can be complicated and a time-drain for employers. Rather than do it by themselves each pay period, many companies outsource the function to streamline the process.

Payroll Register: A document that displays a company's payroll for a specific period. A good payroll register can provide a wealth of information to accountants. Payroll Registers should list the details surrounding each employee's pay for a specific period. They can list employee names, hours worked, gross pay, deductions, net pay, type of pay, and related payroll taxes. Your clients will probably outsource their payroll processing to an outside payroll provider. There are dozens of companies that specialize in payroll processing. Payroll registers will probably be generated by your client through its payroll provider.

PBC: Prepared by Client. You might frequently hear the phrase "PBC list." At the outset of each engagement, your team will put together a PBC list of support needed from your client. This list could become the bane of your client's existence, but it is the list of support your firm must see in order to complete the engagement.

PDW: Per Discussion With. Usually a client contact's name will follow the phase "PDW." It is a shortcut an accountant might use to document who was spoken to about a certain matter.

Picking List: Documents that tell employees the type and quantity of inventory, items, materials, etc., that are needed to complete specific projects or orders. I like to think of them as lists that tell employees which items to "Pick" from the warehouse shelves to fulfill a certain customer order.

PO: Purchase Order. A buyer will usually submit a PO to a seller to officially request a certain order. POs may contain information related to the type of product being ordered, the transaction price, payment terms, the date of the order, shipping terms, and any other information the buyer wishes to send the seller.

POC: Percentage of Completion.

Population: Sets of data that support balances or amounts. For example, if a company completes a control at the end of each month and you need to review one instance of the control during the year, you would have a total population of twelve to choose from. Public accountants frequently select and test samples from populations in order to gain comfort over the entire population. Before you begin making selections from a Population, make sure the total of the Population agrees to the number, balance, or amount you think it should match. Making samples from a bad population is not good, so make sure the total population ties out before proceeding with any further work.

LINGO YOU DIDN'T HEAR IN SCHOOL

PPV: Purchase Price Variance. The PPV is the difference between the actual cost of a good and its standard or estimated cost. For example, if an item had a standard cost of $10 but actually cost $12, the PPV related to the item would be $2.

PY: Prior Year. PY can be used to say the matter, amount, or issue being discussed agrees to prior year.

Reconciliation: Reconciliations (often called "recs" or "recons") document how one number from one file or document ties out to a different number in a different file or document. For a reconciliation to exist, there must be subtractions, add-backs, or some other "reconciling item" needed in order for the two numbers to tie out. Bank account reconciliations, payroll reconciliations, and monthly account reconciliations are some of the major reconciliations performed by accountants. Below I have shown a generic payroll reconciliation so you can see an example reconciliation in action.

Workpaper 1350			
December 31, 2019 Payroll Reconciliation			
Total Payroll Per 2019 Annual Payroll Register			$200.00
Minus: 2018 Payroll Receivable			$-10.00
Plus: 2019 Payroll Receivable			$15.00
Total			$205.00
Total Payroll Expense Per 2019 Trial Balance			$205.00
Difference			$0.00

In the rec above, I show how the $200 of payroll expenses from a company's annual payroll register ties out to the $205 seen on the company's trial balance. Cash and accrual basis differences came into play in this example (the trial balance is on an accrual basis and the payroll register is on a cash basis) so prior year and current receivables had to be factored into the rec to document how the $200 seen on the payroll register agrees to the $205 seen on the trial balance.

Rep Letter: Rep Letter is short for Management Representation Letter.

RIF: Reduction In Force. A RIF is a more pleasant way of saying that employees have been or will be laid off. RIF's can occur due to a reduction in work needed by the employer, a reduction in the funds available for payroll, an M&A event, a restructuring, or another downsizing event. RIF's are typically permanent and replacement hires or re-hires are not typically expected in the months following a RIF.

Roll-Back: A Roll-back is a document that displays how an ending balance "rolls back" to an earlier beginning balance. A Roll-back is the inverse of a roll-forward (see definition below). Roll-backs are commonly related to inventory balances, so I have provided an example inventory Roll-back below.

Workpaper 8000				
12/31/2019 Inventory Roll-back				
Item Name	January 5, 2020 Count Total	Purchases from 1/1/2020-1/5/2020	Sales & Disposals from 1/1/2020-1/5/2020	12/31/2019 Total
Item A	10	3	2	9
Item B	7	5	6	8
Item C	25	6	4	23

To walk-through the example above, let us assume you conducted

LINGO YOU DIDN'T HEAR IN SCHOOL

an inventory count on January 5, 2020 for a client with a December 31, 2019 year-end. You counted 10 Item A's on January 5, 2020, but you actually need to know the number of Item A's that were included in your client's inventory on December 31, 2019 (the year-end date), not January 5, 2020 (your count date). This roll-back shows that 3 Item A's were purchased by your client in the period from December 31, 2019 to January 5, 2020, and 2 Item A's were sold. If you have gathered evidence of these transactions, you can back in to the 9 Item A's that existed in your client's inventory at December 31, 2019. The 9 Item A's are just a function of the number of Item A's you counted on January 5, 2020 and the net effect of the activity between December 31, 2019 and January 5, 2020.

Roll-Forward: A Roll-forward is a document or file showing how one account balance from a period "Rolls-forward" to a new balance in the next period due to client activity or transactions. A common Roll-forward in accounting is the fixed asset Roll-forward. Below is an example that should be easy to follow. Fixed asset Roll-forwards should show the beginning balances of the accounts listed, any additions, any disposals, and the ending balances of the account. Note that ending balances should always be a function of beginning balances and the net effect of any activity during the period the Roll-forward covers.

Workpaper 1900					
2019 Fixed Asset Rollforward					
		January 1, 2019			December 31, 2019
Account Number	Account Name	Beginning Balance	Additions	Disposals	Ending Balance
1200	Computers	$50.00	$25.00	$5.00	$70.00
1300	Furniture	$100.00	$30.00	$50.00	$80.00
1400	Vehicles	$150.00	$50.00	$75.00	$125.00

Roll-Off: To Roll-off is to be reassigned from one engagement or one project to another. Sometimes associates and interns are only scheduled to work on a job or project for a specific period of time. Even if your project is not completed yet, you might be asked to Roll-off in order to work on a different project.

SALY: Same As Last Year. SALY can be used to say the balance, procedure, risk, etc., in the current period is the same as last period.

Selections/Samples: Accountants make Selections (or Samples) from a population to gain a reasonable level of comfort over the population without having to test every data point within the population. As a new associate or intern, you will be responsible for making Selections.

SG&A Expenses: Selling, General, and Administrative Expenses. Companies consistently are looking for ways to trim SG&A expenses without hurting production or output.

Sign Off (a work-paper): In order to catch mistakes and minimize the risk of an error being made, work traditionally is performed and reviewed by separate parties within a firm. For example, an associate typically performs testing (the associate in this case would be known as the "preparer). After the testing is complete, the associate's work will then be reviewed by a senior (in this case this senior would be known as the "first reviewer"). After the senior has reviewed, the testing will be reviewed by a manager ("second reviewer"). After the manager reviews, it will be reviewed by the Partner (the "final reviewer"). When each party either completes or reviews the testing, the party "Signs

Off" on the testing by literally initialing or signing the testing to indicate that it is ready of the next level of review. When a senior asks you if a certain work-paper has been Signed Off on yet, he is asking if it is complete and ready for review.

SKU: Stock Keeping Unit. SKUs are numbers or codes assigned to a product by the product's owner to assist in identifying and organizing the product within the owner's inventory records.

SO: Sales Order. A SO is a form or document issued by a business to its customer to confirm the customer's PO. SOs help the business track and organize the orders it receives from customers. POs usually trigger the creation of SOs, and each SO should list the corresponding PO that triggered its creation. The SO might list the quantity of goods or services ordered, the price, the date of order and delivery, shipping terms, and payment terms. SOs can provide a goldmine of data.

SOW: Statement of Work. Think of a SOW as a description of the work one party will do for another party, similar to a contract between two parties.

SOX: Sarbanes-Oxley.

Sub: Subsidiary. When company A buys company B, company B becomes a Sub of company A. In this situation company A is company B's parent or holding company. A Sub is a separate legal entity from its parent company. The parent company acquires liability protection due to the legal separation.

Support: Support is the evidence gathered to "support" financial data. Support can consist of check copies, invoices, contracts, bank statements, physical observations, analytics, employee HR records, and a plethora of other files. Support is gathered, documented, and reviewed for firm liability purposes. It will be used as evidence to "support" your firm's final opinion or deliverable.

TB: Trial Balance. I like to think of the TB as the backbone of all of accounting projects. The numbers found in the TB will be the numbers your firm ultimately is engaged to opine on (audit) or work with (tax and advisory).

TCJA: Tax Cuts and Jobs Act of 2017.

Tie Out: A tie out is the act of agreeing information or data from one file, document, or work-paper to another. Often accountants look to ensure the same number or piece of data is shown in separate files, documents, or work-papers. To tie out a number is to document that a number shown in one document is also found in another document. This is a term that is easy to understand when seen in use, so I have put a screenshot of a tie out below to better illustrate the meaning. When you tie out a number from one document (A) to a single page within another multi-page document (B), tie out the number to the specific page number in the multi-page document (B) so your reviewer has an easier time locating the number within the multi-page document. As a reviewer, scanning through a thousand-page pdf in search of a single tie out can be infuriating. Numbers between two files usually do not have to agree to the penny in order for your firm to show they agree.

LINGO YOU DIDN'T HEAR IN SCHOOL

Depending on the project's materiality and designated trivial levels, slight variances can be acceptable between the two numbers or data points you are attempting to tie out. If you see a small difference, your firm will probably want you to calculate the difference somewhere on the work-paper and mark it as immaterial.

Workpaper 1215
December 31, 2019 Prepaid Expense Listing

Name	Date	Vendor	Amount	
Prepaid #1	12/22/2019	Vendor A	$5.00	
Prepaid #2	12/24/2019	Vendor B	$10.00	
Prepaid #3	12/26/2019	Vendor C	$10.00	
Prepaid #4	12/28/2019	Vendor D	$15.00	
Total Prepaid Expenses - Account 3000			$40.00	1100

Workpaper 1100
December 31, 2019 Trial Balance - Assets

Account Number	Account Name	Account Balance	
1000	Cash	$20.00	
2000	Accounts Receivable	$20.00	
3000	Prepaid Expenses	$40.00	1215
4000	Fixed Assets	$20.00	
Total Assets		$100.00	

In the screenshot of a tie out seen above, the preparer has tied out a $40 total prepaid expense balance from a prepaid expense listing to a $40 prepaid balance seen on the trial balance. Your firm will probably give each work-paper a work-paper number for storage and reference purposes. Each of the work-paper numbers seen above are used to document that the $40 balance is also seen in the other work-paper. The viewer of the prepaid expense listing at work-paper 1215 can see the $40 total balance agrees to the trial balance at work-paper 1100, and the viewer of work-paper 1100 can see the $40 prepaid expense balance agrees to the prepaid expense listing at work-paper 1215.

TM: Tick-mark. Tick-marks are shorthand markings used by accountants to add a further explanation to documentation or to quickly show that certain procedures have been conducted. Using tick-marks instead of writing documentation out can save massive amounts of time and energy. Your firm will probably have a proprietary set of tick-marks it uses to denote common actions taken on work-papers. As a new associate or intern, make a tick-mark bank by writing down the meanings of all tick-marks that are unfamiliar to you for your future reference. If you create this bank it should not take more than a week or two to learn the meanings of all of your firm's tick-marks.

WFI: Waive Further Investigation. You will often see this abbreviation at the end of a work-paper to indicate the work-paper preparer has gathered enough support in the course of testing to gain comfort over the data.

WFH and Working Remotely: Working From Home. You might receive a message in an email from your manager similar to, "I am WFH today, but don't hesitate to email me with any questions."

Work-Paper: Work-papers are the files and documents public accountants conduct their work upon. Work-papers can come in all sorts of shapes, sizes, and formats. When I first began my career, I mistakenly assumed that all work-papers had to come in the same, standard format. This was a totally incorrect assumption. There is no one-size-fits-all style to work-papers. Each work-paper's appearance will be the result of the client, the support, and the work to be performed in the work-paper.

YE: Year-End. Often you will see the phrase "at YE." This just means "at Year-End." YE is usually the date of the client balance sheet.

YTD: Year To Date. It means the time period between the beginning of the fiscal year and the last date (which has occurred) that is still within the fiscal year. If you are working on a December 31, 2010 year-end client and today is June 30, 2010, YTD would cover the period from January 1, 2010 to June 30, 2010. If today is August 1, 2010, YTD would cover the period from January 1 to August 1, 2010. If today is February 1, 2011, YTD 2010 would cover the period from January 1, 2010 to December 31, 2010.

You will not be a fully functioning associate after reviewing these terms, but you will definitely be headed in the right direction. You will be able to ask better questions, feel more confident in your ability to complete the task at hand, and will become more proficient at your job. It will be hard to complete many tasks without knowing the meanings of the unique terms and phrases your firm uses. Remember, you can't reach your final destination if you can't read your map, so try your best to not just memorize but actually understand these terms and their meanings as you begin your career.

FAREWELL

I hope you have enjoyed this book as much as I have enjoyed writing it. If you have any comments, criticisms, suggestions, or compliments regarding my thoughts and opinions, I would love to hear them at bonanzafeedback1@gmail.com. I hope you now feel like you have some tips and tricks to use to accelerate your career development. Thank you again for your purchase of this book, and I wish you the best of luck as you begin your career.

www.ingramcontent.com/pod-product-compliance
Lightning Source LLC
Chambersburg PA
CBHW020442110526
44587CB00038B/928